TRANSITION
AMERICA

TRANSITION AMERICA

Dr. David Garrahan

Library of Congress Control Number: 2016914594
ISBN: Hardcover   978-1-5245-4034-0
                 Softcover   978-1-5245-4032-6
                 eBook   978-1-5245-4033-3

Rev. date: 09/01/2016

To order additional copies of this book, contact:
Xlibris
1-888-795-4274
www.Xlibris.com
Orders@Xlibris.com
734142

CONTENTS

The author shows his granddaughter
the World Trade Center and
how great America is.
Several weeks later, they were gone,
and America was forever changed.

US Senator Orrin Hatch congratulates the author.

To Erika and Jack

INTRODUCTION

Try not to cast the book aside because the recommendations are too radical. When Americans are fearful of visiting Disney World with their children; do not gather at a 4th of July celebration; avoid their favorite restaurants; and imagine their priest being beheaded on the altar –it is time to think outside the box for guidance.

In this book, I address the serious primary issues facing our government and the American people and put forth proposals to correct the misguided path that our nation is on. Attention is focused on the economy, national security and terrorism, health care, education, and a foreign policy that shapes our military strategy. This is a formidable undertaking, as each of these issues is properly the subject for an entire book.

The economy is in a precarious position. Today's growing federal debt is $19,408,405,433,921.[1] Terrorist attacks threaten us at home and abroad. Health care is not as available as Americans were led to believe. Education is in decline at every level. Our foreign policy misguides the nation's military strategy. The United States is on the verge of rekindling the Cold War with Russia. Terrorist attacks have begun to strike within homeland America.

The greatest threat to the American people is the federal government, which has grown to a size that renders it unmanageable and largely unaccountable. The Obama administration's regulations have filled 468,500 pages in the Federal Register.[2] There are several hundred agencies, bureaus, and institutes. The US Office of Personnel Management reports that there were 2,726,000 federal civilian employees as of 2014.[3]

With all these agencies and departments, the government is so dysfunctional that in 2016, children in Flint, Michigan, are drinking lead-poisoned water, and a US Hellfire missile sent to Europe for NATO training purposes was wrongly shipped to Cuba.[4] The United States continues to lose the respect of world leaders. Congress is too often not able to enact legislation. Elected politicians fail to honor their promises to reform and downsize government.

Americans are frustrated and angry. Some are becoming frightened, hunkering down, and buying guns before the erosion of the second amendment. Gun sales reached the highest level on record in 2015.[5] Fortunately, there has also been an increase in voter turnout in the presidential primaries. And the fact that so many voters are casting their ballots for Donald Trump and Bernie Sanders is sending shock waves through the political establishment. The Republican Party power brokers are frantic in their efforts to deny Trump the nomination. The Democratic Party leaders are comfortable in believing that the voters will not elect a self-described "democratic socialist" and that Clinton will not be indicted.

In the following chapters, I will address in detail the foregoing problems and challenges facing America. They do not lend themselves to easy solutions. Each has a history of resistance to change and a trail of failed efforts at reform. Readers will note that throughout the book, several themes resurface. For the most part, this is a reflection of the interrelatedness of the problems, and at other points it is for additional emphasis. The solutions will not be easy, and most will be vehemently resisted. Some readers may judge the proposals set forth in the following chapters to be perfunctory or even impossible to implement. However, for most concerned readers, there is sufficient direction for them to envision the transition from the current condition to a profoundly better government and a better future for all Americans.

I am not a historian, economist, security expert, or military strategist.[6] Accordingly, to avoid complexities beyond my expertise, certain simplifications are used, which I judged to be essentially unimportant so far as my purpose in writing the book was concerned. My intended readership is the American people, the electorate. I have no interest in influencing your vote. My interest is in encouraging every citizen to exercise their right, if not duty, to vote. I did not enjoy the luxury of time, since I deemed it important to get the book out well in advance of the very important November election.

Readers are encouraged to read the referenced endnotes. Most are "open source" or in the public domain. You can easily google these references and read the detailed sourced material. I tried to place relevant personal information in the endnotes so as to not detract from the substance of the text. They do provide important context for my thinking and the positions that I take on issues and solutions.

So set the smartphone aside for a while. Read *Transition America*. Regardless of your politics, you will be glad that you did.

CHAPTER ONE

America in Decline

America is in a state of decline. Politicians, government officials, and federal bureaucrats have slowly eroded the underpinnings of our democracy, marriage and family, work, education, and free enterprise capitalism. Americans are facing unprecedented challenges on several fronts. There is widespread concern about terrorism within our borders and armed conflict abroad, our economic recovery, underemployment, undereducation, overtaxation, a staggering national debt, a failure of leadership, a dysfunctional congress, and a government grown so large that it is unmanageable and unable to serve the needs of the people.

Our federal government is broken, and all three branches have fallen victim. The legislative branch, Congress, is not only hopelessly divided politically, but one can barely discern the difference between the Republicans and Democrats. The executive branch has become overly politicized. This could hardly have been more evident than the immediate conflict with Congress after the untimely death of Supreme Court Justice Scalia. And the judicial branch itself, beginning with the aborted nomination of

Robert Bork, has become increasingly political in the exercise of its constitutional duty.

Facing a world of conflict, disorder, and rapid radical change, our government struggles as it seeks to find direction and stability. Many believe that it is beyond self-repair. It no longer represents the will of the people and is incapable/unwilling to address the widespread concerns of the electorate. The US Senate, long viewed with respect as the legislative branch's deliberate body and a model of civil discourse, has now been reduced to the point of a senator calling a colleague a liar in open session. In the House, the condition is still worse as pending bills are typically stalled and languish in committee. It is my studied judgment that America needs a new political party that actually listens to the people, one that has empathy for the people, a People's Party.

The American economy is in recovery, but the national debt of over nineteen trillion dollars is a huge threat to the economy and the country. We appear to not learn from our own mistakes or the mistakes that have trashed the economies of Japan, Greece, Brazil, and Argentina. The Bank of Japan recently blindsided global financial markets by adopting negative interest rates, buckling under pressure to revive growth in the world's third-largest economy.[7] The European Central Bank is considering enacting a zero-interest rate. The United States is attempting to normalize interest rates, which many observers believe have been held too low for too long. While it is clear that the economy is moving into a recovery mode after the years of monetary easing and stimulation, there is some concern about inflation, and the debt level is a serious threat to the economy. The Bureau of Labor Statistics reports an unemployment rate below 5 percent. I suspect it may be closer to double that number.

We need to stimulate the economy by creating real jobs and raise wages that will increase consumer spending. We should capitalize on our newfound natural gas and oil resources. While there are individuals who will never be comfortable with fracking, in the past five years, the industry has vastly improved fracking technology. However, the industry should redirect itself to remediate the legitimate issues related to offshore drilling. The Arctic and federal land in Alaska hold vast undeveloped oil reserves and untapped gas reserves. The challenge in recovering these resources lies in the development of offshore drilling technology. The industry must reduce drilling risk to an acceptable level and likewise develop new cleanup methods so as to ameliorate the environmental impact. The proper recovery of these resources would have a significant impact on the economy and free us from our dependency relationship with Saudi Arabia.

Previously, it was noted that the national debt, as distinct from the national deficit, is a treat to our future. The deficit is of considerably less concern as it is a measure of a single year's budgetary shortfall. The government needs to continue to reduce annual spending while tapping new sources of revenue. The nineteen-trillion-dollar national debt, however, is increasing 2.4 billion dollars every day[8] (see appendix A). Congress refuses to recognize that we lost the war on poverty and continues to fund counterproductive programs and creates additional entitlements. Health care and social security costs continue to burden the economy. In subsequent chapters, I will address these critical issues and put forth strategies and specific proposals and recommendations that will eliminate the national debt in the not-too-distant future.

Americans need to recognize that the condition of the economy is a direct result of decision making by elected politicians and federal officials. Government, then, is the primary threat that must be addressed. It has grown to the point of dysfunction. The federal government is in decline. For decades, politicians have promised to rein in government spending and reduce the size of big government. Unfortunately, they have not fulfilled these pledges. They are more concerned with their own power and enrichment than they are with addressing the needs of the people.

"Pork" spending by Congress has exploded in recent years. "Pork" and "earmarks" are similar concepts. They refer to money set aside by legislators for projects in their home states. Readers may be familiar with some of these pork projects: $250,000 for sidewalk repair in Boca Raton, Florida, $100,000 for a film festival in Rochester, New York, $350,000 for the Rock and Roll Hall of Fame in Cleveland, Ohio.[9] We generally think of Republicans as fiscal conservatives. They are as guilty of pork barrel politics as the Democrats. It is corrupt. It appears that they spend more time on earmarking legislation than they do on studying the federal budget.

Our elected officials have politicized the Supreme Court and the Justice Department. A steady stream of executive orders has caused disruption to the balance of powers in government. Several of these orders are currently being tested in the courts and will likely end up before the Supreme Court. The US Constitution has been repeatedly ignored and thereby weakened. Many of the federal agencies, bureaus, and departments have also been politicized. Most readers are familiar with the scandalous conditions plaguing the Department of Veterans Affairs (VA) and the Internal Revenue Service (IRS). Both are suspected of serious misdeeds of a criminal nature, followed by layers of cover-up and denial. One recent example, the VA created a system intended to solve the problem of their continuing to send payment checks to dead people, but it resulted in the VA declaring 4,201 people dead who were alive and not receiving their benefit checks. The VA's published statistics over the past forty years reveal that an average of twenty two military veterans commit suicide every day in the U.S. Still there is no accountability. The Environmental Protection Agency (EPA) has exceeded its authority in regulating and crippling private industry, and will be addressed in chapter five.

There have been more than 25,000 regulations issued during the Obama administration. In fairness, it should be noted that this proliferation is not out of line with previous administrations. These thousands of regulations must be widely distributed for proper implementation and enforcement. The government employs a huge contingent of workers just to manage the records of these regulations. The economy has been choked by thousands of complicated and unnecessary regulations that are dealing a threatening strike at our democracy. If left unchecked, the consequences for future generations will be dire. I am reminded of Barry Goldwater's statement: "I fear Washington and centralized government more than I do Moscow." While sourcing Goldwater's quote, I happened upon Charles Koch's: "No centralized government, no matter how big, how smart, or how powerful, can effectively and efficiently control much of society in a beneficial way. On the contrary, big governments are inherently inefficient and harmful."[10] Americans need to declare war on our out-of-control big government and the uncontrolled spending of their money. Politics and government are in decline.

The American culture is in decline. We are experiencing a decline in our indigenous American population as families are becoming smaller. Our uncontrolled borders have encouraged an influx of immigrants who typically have larger families and typically do not use the English language. The English language is in decline. The bedrock of our nation rested on the belief in marriage and family, religion, and work, all of which are evolving. We are witnessing a rapid decline in our values and mores. The moral fabric of our belief system is changing. The value of a cohesive family and fatherhood is changing.

Education in America is in decline. This problem will be covered in detail in chapter 6. For now, suffice it to state that we are witnessing a dumbing down in American education at all levels. More than 25 percent of students fail to graduate high school in four years. For Hispanic, Native American, and African American students, the percentages are significantly higher. This trend is very troubling for many obvious reasons. Most readers will recognize that this trend impedes socioeconomic mobility. This is the case because of the significant correlation between level of education and level of income. The inability to move from one economic level or social position to another is fraught with undesirable consequences.[11] Education is the linchpin to socioeconomic mobility. With education in decline, social and economic mobility are in decline. America is in decline. If any group suffers and does not have equal access to education and social/economic mobility, the nation suffers decline.

After World War II, Europe was a wasteland of broken countries. There was a need to restore international law and stability. The United States stepped forward. American think tanks composed of intellectuals, former diplomats, and entrepreneurial leaders refined the Greek principle of hegemony, which espouses the political, economic, or military predominance or control by one country over others.[12] Sparta and Athens each assumed the role of hegemon. Believing that American hegemony would be beneficial to democracy and development, most nations endorsed this role for the United States. The USSR did not, which was perceived as a sign of their aggressive intentions. Seventy years later, liberals and academics continue to defend hegemony. They ignore the fact that American efforts to maintain order (Afghanistan, Libya, Iraq, Somalia, et al.) have been a primary source of disorder in the international system.

Reich and Lebow's scholarly and insightful production provides a theoretical basis to frame the primary thesis of this book, which is the pressing need for the United States to reset its foreign policy and promote a multipolar world order. [13] However, I differ with those who would have us abandon our position of leadership and influence. The United States has shouldered the burden of hegemon. Economically, politically, and morally. America can no longer afford to be this type of world leader. Many believe that the United States is no longer a good leader. We have lost respect and influence. Even long-standing allies are beginning to look elsewhere for direction and leadership. The manner in which we have exercised our military power around the globe has effectively diminished our standing and influence. In the twenty-first century, there are better ways to influence, if not lead, the state of world affairs.

Krauthammer states that "two decades into the unipolar world that came about with the fall of the Soviet Union, America is in the position of deciding whether to abdicate or retain its dominance . . . facing the choice of whether to maintain our dominance or to gradually, deliberately, willingly, and indeed relievedly give it up, we are currently on a course towards the latter."[14]

I agree that the United States is drifting away from its unipolar position of dominance. But rather than drift into a role that is effectively being defined by other nation states and external forces, I believe that it is imperative that America define the terms of its disengagement, control its own destiny, and do so in its own time. We can exercise leadership by other than military means. Think of it as soft power. The United States must always maintain its military superiority and make it obvious to China, Iran, North Korea, and Russia. We should, however, retain our role on the world stage through economic, diplomatic, sociopolitical, and moral leadership. We will support international institutions and alliances. We will foster a natural multipolar international system of law, order, and stability. Our role on the world stage ought to be carefully redefined by Americans by resetting our nation's foreign policy and refocusing our military. It can be accomplished without fear of precipitating global turmoil. It is no longer in our national interest to stay the course. We need to stop America's decline in the world and do it on our terms—transition America.

CHAPTER TWO

Global Turmoil and America's Role

Global tensions have become increasingly disruptive. Witness the strife in the Middle East, in Europe, in North Africa. Observe the escalating disorder in Yemen, Libya, Nigeria, Somalia, and Sudan. Armed conflict continues in Iraq and Syria. Afghanistan suffers from long-standing tribal discord and a resurgence of the Taliban. Saudi Arabia is again threatening Iran, as Iran tests intercontinental ballistic missiles capable of mounting nuclear warheads. Meanwhile, Japan and the Philippines have joined with Vietnam in expressing outrage at China over the construction of airfields and military facilities in the Spratly Islands. The United States has said that China broke a pledge not to militarize the disputed islands. It has become increasingly clear that China intends to continue this territorial expansion. It views the U.S. as a 'paper tiger' that is outwardly powerful, but inwardly ineffectual… the European Union and NATO are preoccupied with terror attacks, and Russia may even join China in this territorial claim. As long as Cambodia stays aligned with China, the southeast asian nations are stymied and China will stay its course.

Russia has not satisfied its appetite in Ukraine with the illegal annexation of Crimea. It will continue to seize control, occupy by proxy, and attempt other annexations of territory belonging to sovereign countries. North Korea is testing hydrogen devices, as it threatens its neighbors, as well as the United States. North Korea's top military body said recently that it was prepared to make a preemptive nuclear strike on the US mainland.[15] Such aggressive rhetoric is common from supreme leader Kim Jong-un. He is immature, unstable, and dangerous and should be taken out. Unfortunately, the CIA has been denied that prerogative.

Given the United States' intrusion in Korea, Vietnam, Iraq, Afghanistan, Libya, et al., we could have assassinated these leaders and thereby have spared the lives of well over one hundred thousand young Americans on foreign soil. The point is made in chapters 3 and 4 that we should never have placed American troops in any of these foreign countries.

There is no hint of progress in a two-state solution to the Israeli-Palestinian conflict, which dates to the late 1800s when Zionists immigrated to Palestine in search of a Jewish state. The indigenous population became alarmed, and eventually, fighting broke out.[16] This is an oversimplification of a very long-standing, complex issue. Israel has put forth numerous proposals over the years, even making a complete and painful withdrawal from Gaza in 2005—to no avail. Meanwhile, there is ongoing tension between mostly Hindu India and mostly Muslim Pakistan over the disputed Kashmir region. Both nations have nuclear capability. In January 2016, six terrorists crossed the border into India and launched a massive assault on the airbase in Pathankot.[17] Evidence did link the attack to a terror group and not to state action. The problem, however, continues to simmer.

Syria is a tragedy of untold magnitude against humanity. The crisis was fueled four years ago when the United States decided to back the rebels by supplying them with weapons to fight President Bashar Assad. More than 430,000 people have been killed and more than eleven million displaced and suffering terrible consequences of this war, now in its fifth year. On February 12, 2016, Assad said that he intends to retake the whole country from rebel forces.[18] Tensions are mounting, as Saudi Arabia, Iran, and Russia are now participants in the civil war in Syria. The refugees fleeing this war have precipitated a crisis in the European Union, which previously had enjoyed open borders.

It has been reported that Germany took in 1.1 million migrants in 2015.[19] This uncontrolled mass migration, primarily from war-torn Syria, has created huge problems for member states of the European Union. In addition to the economic and logistic issues in accommodating millions of refugees entering rapidly and the reality that some Islamic radicals have entered Europe as migrants, it must be recognized that there are differences between the belief systems of the majority of migrants and of the Western culture of the European Union. There is an element of incompatibility between Islam and Western democracy dating back centuries. The Ottomans refused to accept European states as either legitimate or equal. And Kissinger traces this divide to the doorstep of the twenty-first century.[20]

It is important to realize that Christianity and Islam have intermittently battled each other for 1,200 years, beginning with the Crusades and the campaign to expel Muslims from southern Iberia.[21] Beginning in 1983, the United States has sent military forces into four mainly Muslim countries. Lebanon, Libya, Iraq, and Somalia were targeted for American intervention.[22] Subsequently, the World Trade Center in Manhattan experienced its first terrorist attack. In June 1993, Sheik Omar Abdel-Rahman, a blind cleric, was arrested, along with a number of the members of a New Jersey mosque where he preached and charged with conspiring to commit acts of terrorism.[23] One can see evidence of a relational linkage between US military interventions in Muslim countries and the beginning of terrorism in America. It could be argued that the United States fanned the flames of the Arab Spring, even encouraging the toppling of regimes, several of which were the region's most stable leaders. There is a trail that passes through Tunisia, Egypt, Libya, Yemen, Iraq, Somalia, and other countries where covert American activity is typically identifiable years after the fact.

In the following pages, I will present an abbreviated but fact-specific overview of US military and intelligence activity around the world during the past fifty years. An understanding of this American interventionist history will form a foundation for chapters 3 and 4 and may soften the impact of the series of proposals put forth in those chapters that some readers will judge to be radical and naive.

Recall that the U.S. declared 'war on terror' in 2001. To date we have not won the war. In fact, Americans are less safe today than they were fifteen years ago. There are two viable solutions to solving the problem of terrorism which will be detailed in the following chapters.

Understanding recent history will explain why so many good Muslims despise Americans; some hate us, as their behavior demonstrates. I will begin with Iran because the facts are now available. The intelligence community previously denied these facts. In 1953, the Central Intelligence Agency developed a plan to depose Iran's prime minister, Mohammad Mosaddegh, and secretly planned with their British counterpart a coup d'état. The

United States had covert agents inside Iran engaged in nefarious activity to operationalize the plan. Mosaddegh's government fell to the conspirators in August 1953. The coup's reverberations have haunted its orchestrators over the years. Marking the sixtieth anniversary of the overthrow of the Iranian prime minister, the National Security Archive, on August 19, 2013, released declassified but heavily redacted documents that provide new specifics. For example, Kermit Roosevelt was the senior CIA officer on the ground in Iran who directed the overthrow. It was he who coordinated the activities of US and British agents and directed payments to tribesmen who played a key role in the plot against Mohammad Mosaddegh.[24]

The United States continued to meddle in Iranian affairs into the 1960s and 1970s when the Ayatollah Khomeini publicly and bitterly attacked the shah for unleashing his forces against the clergy. Our government flew the shah to the United States presumably for medical care. Many Iranians rejected this explanation, believing instead that the Americans were preparing to restore the shah to the throne as they had done in 1953. In a defining moment, Iranian students occupied the American embassy in Tehran and held US diplomats hostage until Ronald Reagan was inaugurated in January 1981 (in the interim, President Carter authorized a botched rescue attempt).

Similarly, the United States has been meddling in Syrian affairs for years.[25] Many of the covert operations failed to achieve their goals; some were counterproductive, driving leaders further into the arms of the plotters' adversaries, and with time, Middle Eastern regimes learned to fight back, frequently employing the weapon of state-sponsored, though typically deniable, terrorism. Regarding the question of what turned Syria toward the Soviet

Union, Rathwell concludes that the root causes lay in the anticommunism of the Eisenhower administration.[26]

There is documented evidence of the United States' covert involvement in regime-change operations in Guatemala, Chad, Lebanon, Nicaragua, Pakistan, Chile, Congo, and other sovereign countries.[27,28] The goal of the US government was to democratize and/or facilitate leadership transitions in these sovereign nations and thereby establish regimes that would be beholden to the United States. The facts relative to these intrusions are now indisputable. Clearly, this was the exercise of raw power by the United States as the acknowledged leader of a unipolar world. It was an egregious abuse of American power then, and it continues to be an abuse of American power now in the Middle East and Africa. The tragic consequences then and now are obvious.

The United States has left a trail, frequently difficult to discern, of toppled leaders and destruction in foreign lands. The National Security Archive reported minutes of meetings between State Department and CIA officials and summaries of covert US action in Chile between 1970 and 1973. They show specific efforts to destabilize Chile economically and to isolate Allende's government diplomatically. These official documents detail the military coup led by General Pinochet (with US support), which toppled the democratically elected socialist Popular Unity government of Salvador Allende, who died of a self-inflicted gunshot as a backed US military coup converged on his presidential palace. US State Department and National Security Council memoranda and cables following the coup provide evidence of the egregious human rights atrocities under President Pinochet's military government.[29] The United States orchestrated this sordid affair.

The United States' efforts to democratize Nicaragua had been in place for many years when we covertly funded the rebel Contras in an operation later referred to as the Iran-Contra affair. Under President Reagan the U.S. supplied weapons and money to the Contras. In 1985, the U.S. provided over $35 million in 'non-lethal' aid to the rebel Contra forces. Yet, in 2016, Daniel Ortega is still in place promoting his brand of communism and considerable financial corruption. This is another failed American intervention. The Monroe Doctrine has been used as a premise for more than one hundred years to justify U.S. intervention in Central America.

The United States has a bad track record in its support of dictators around the globe. The shah of Iran was our man. We supported Saddam Hussein in Iraq until we stopped supporting him. The United States supported General Pervez Musharraf in Pakistan as he seized control through a military coup d'état in 1999. He was subsequently charged with high treason for having implemented emergency rules and suspending the constitution. The United States undermined Hosni Mubarak in Egypt, and the aftermath was bloody. And yet the United States soon began to actively undermine Bashar Assad in Syria, which has resulted in 430,000 civilian deaths and the flight of millions of refugees to Europe. It is understandable why so many Muslims hate Americans. It is understandable why Americans are suffering with terrorism at home and abroad. One could argue that there is at least a correlation between these historical interventions and the ongoing attacks against Americans. The following examples will illustrate the point:

Date	Location	Details
1979	Iran	US embassy attacked; American hostages held for 444 days
1983	Beirut, Lebanon	US military barracks attacked; 241 Americans killed
1988	Libya admits role	Pan Am Flight 103 explodes; 262 fatalities
1993	NYC World Trade Center	Car bomb; 6 Americans killed and over 1,000 injured
1995	Saudi Arabia	Car bomb kills 5 US military personnel
1996	Saudi Arabia	Khobar Towers, truck bomb kills 19 US military personnel
2000	Yemen	US warship *Cole* attacked; 17 American sailors killed
2001	NYC World Trade Center and the Pentagon	Terrorist-hijacked planes crash into World Trade Center and the Pentagon, killing 2,996 people and injuring more than 6,000
2012	Benghazi, Libya	Diplomatic American compound attacked; 4 Americans killed

There are many who believe that the United States has the responsibility to defend not only America but also scores of countries around the globe. In today's international environment, the costs to merely maintain the status quo are growing more onerous, not less. And they fall almost entirely on the backs of US taxpayers and US troops.[30] It is absolutely not in the national interest of the United States to interfere in the internal affairs of sovereign countries.

The United States has been the world's leader, a superpower since the end of World War II. In the past several years, there has been more discussion about the future of US power and leadership. Salvatore Babones writes: "American hegemony is now as firm as, or firmer than, it has ever been and will remain so for a long time to come . . . The United States possesses near-total control of the world's seas, skies, airwaves, and cyberspace, while American universities, think tanks and journals dominate the world of ideas."[31] This writer, however, believes that American hegemony is in decline. We have lost respect around the world and are perceived as a world leader because of our economic and military power and our continued willingness to dispense money in the form of foreign aid around the globe. It is not in America's interest to continue down this path. The US government and the American people need to begin reconceptualizing the nation's role in the world before it is too late, and our role is defined by others. We ought not to obsess about how other nations view us. We have the comfort of knowing that we will always remain a military superpower, and this strength provides us the opportunity to reassess our role in the world and redefine American leadership.

Krauthammer writes that "if one's foreign policy is to reject the very notion of international primacy in the first place, a domestic agenda that takes away the resources to maintain such primacy in perfectly complementary. Indeed, the two are synergistic . . . our interventionist tradition is recent. Our isolationist tradition goes far deeper." And later he cites Jeane Kirkpatrick (US ambassador to the United Nations during the Reagan administration) in 1990, "It is time to give up the dubious benefits of superpower status . . . time to give up the 'unusual burdens' of the past, and 'return to 'normal' times."[32] I believe that the American people and our nation are best served by having America transition from its primacy role in the world. This is not to suggest an abdication of leadership responsibility. The United States will continue to lead the world as it influences direction using economic, sociopolitical, cultural, intellectual/educational vehicles. The means will be cooperation, collaboration, competition, and at times, coercion, particularly in the economic arena. The United States will continue to support the International Monetary Fund and the World Bank. On the humanitarian front, we will join other nations in promoting the mission of the World Health Organization. America will showcase its culture through participation in the International Arts & Artists organization. The United States will participate in other multilateral international organizations, including the G7 (Group of Seven) and the G20.

The United States will always stand ready to receive refugees from every country in distress. They will complete an entrance application written in their respective native language, and be vetted by the Department of Homeland Security. Upon acceptance, they will be placed in a welcoming community and provided with transitional support as they achieve independence and become contributing members of a great nation. The U.S. can accommodate tens of thousands of vetted refugees. It will be good for them and for America.

America's timely, self-directed transition into a multipolar world will require a strong US economy. And our government must take action to eradicate the national debt. Accordingly, I will now begin to propose several foreign policy initiatives that will serve the twofold purpose of foreign US military disengagement and the development of American economic security. In short, the United States will be redirecting our resources from global expenditures into meeting our demanding internal priorities. This will be challenging. The dialogue must begin now because the alternative of staying the course will cripple America. If one extrapolates from our nation's present condition into the not-so-distant future (that is, if our government remains on its current trajectory), we will soon diminish our military force, further weaken our economy, continue to lose respect and standing in the world, and more violent acts of terrorism will strike Americans at home and abroad.

Uncomfortable questions must be raised. The American people must have a voice in their future, especially since they alone pay the bill with taxpayer dollars. The following dollar amounts are continually increasing, and it is not materially relevant whether the figure is twenty-four billion dollars or thirty-five billion dollars in the present context. Is it in our national interest to spend thirty-four billion dollars on economic aid to more than 150 foreign countries every year? Does the United States need to staff and maintain 294 physical embassies, consulates, and diplomatic posts around the world? Why do we need to staff and maintain eight hundred military bases and facilities in foreign countries? Does the United States still need to maintain forty-eight thousand troops, forty thousand military dependents, and five thousand civilian personnel in Japan in 2017 or thirty-seven thousand troops in Germany and twenty-eight thousand American troops in South Korea? Is it in our national interest to maintain thousands of American troops and CIA personnel in Africa and the Middle East? Neither the State Department nor the Pentagon is asking these questions. American citizens are paying these bills, and they have the right to have answers to these questions.

The world is undergoing transformative change. To what extent does 2016 communication technology inform us about the need to staff and protect 294 diplomatic facilities around the world? Surely, the "diplomatic pouch" has been rendered obsolete. Unlike in 1990, we now have the advantage of digital videoconferencing, smartphones, and encrypted communication transmission. This technology provides for instant global communication. The United States can physically place a government official in any foreign capital within twenty-four hours. The role of the embassy has diminished over recent years as a result of dramatic improvements in travel and communication.[33] [34] Many traditional functions of an embassy can now be executed effectively online. The Obama administration opened a virtual embassy in Iran in 2011 capable of being viewed in both English and Persian.[35] Though it has not been fully embraced by Tehran, it does demonstrate that virtual embassies in selected regions of the world can be instituted effectively.

There are more compelling reasons to close diplomatic posts. We know about the 1979 attack on our embassy in Tehran. More recently, we observed the tragedy at our diplomatic post in Benghazi. Violence against Americans abroad has been increasing, particularly on US government targets.[36] The security environment overseas is dangerous, with numerous extremist groups seeking to target US interests. There were thirteen attacks on US embassies and sixty fatalities during the recent Bush administration. Other US diplomatic posts have been attacked in Saudi Arabia, Kuwait, Greece, Serbia, Yemen, and Uzbekistan as well as in Karachi, Damascus, Beirut, and Baghdad. It makes sense to begin scaling back our physical diplomatic facilities and reduce the number of American targets around the world. The reduction of diplomatic posts should flow from a carefully prioritized list and be executed in an orderly manner. All the physical structures and most of the equipment and vehicles should become the property of the host countries. There will be pockets of resistance. Critics will be quick to label this thinking as a retreat to isolationism. More properly, these changes and the subsequent reductions in the US global footprint should be seen as the beginning of a transition to a noninterventionist foreign policy strategy. It is appropriate to begin reducing the American presence in the Middle East, Asia, and Africa, particularly in predominantly Muslim countries. The following list of diplomatic physical facilities that are no longer in America's interest is put forth as a starting point:

Somalia	Yemen
Nigeria	Sudan
Uganda	Bahrain
Algeria	Libya
Tunisia	Burkina Faso
Lebanon	Chad
Cameroon	Egypt (Alexandria)
Iraq (Kirkuk)	Vietnam (Ho Chi Minh City)
Mozambique	Indonesia (Surabaya)
Afghanistan (Herat)	Saudi Arabia (Dhahran and Jeddah)

A more difficult initiative will be to reduce the total burden of US financial aid and military aid to foreign countries. For too long, our government has caused foreign countries to become dependent on the United States, and this has had the effect of stifling their own development. These dependency relationships are not unlike the debilitating dependency relationships that the federal government has inadvertently created among our African American and Native American populations over the past hundred and fifty years. Many of these foreign countries resent Americans; some encourage the burning of the American flag. These foreign countries are better served if they deal with their rebel groups, safeguard their own borders against transgressions, foster a robust work ethic, and learn to function within the limits of their own resources.

Federal data shows that $37.9 billion was budgeted for foreign aid in fiscal year 2016 and that 34 billion is planned for 2017.[37] At the end of 2015, the American national debt was $18.14 trillion. The United States owes China well over a trillion dollars. The United States gives three billion dollars to Israel. Americans work and send money to the US Treasury. Some argue that the golden era of overseas aid is over. Even in several other countries, the financial climate is now a lot more hostile, and politicians in rich countries are finding it hard to justify spending more on poor people in poor countries when they are cutting spending on poor people at home.[38] And still others believe that there is too much waste and corruption involved in US overseas aid. There are media reports of ongoing corruption involving American monies in Kabul, Afghanistan. The *Washington Post* reported that the United States spent forty-three million dollars to construct a natural gas filling station in Afghanistan.[39] Cut the forty-three million dollars in half. It is still way too much, and I have not read of any person involved being demoted or fired. The West spent $2.3 trillion and still has not managed to get bed nets to poor families or inexpensive medicine or water-purification provisions to those in need.[40]

The respected Pew Global Attitudes Project has been collecting data from residents in foreign countries for more than fifteen years. The countries with the highest percent of citizens who consider the United States an enemy include several NATO partners such as Turkey and Greece. Pakistan and Egypt each receive approximately a billion dollars in US aid each year, and yet 64 percent of the Pakistanis and 26 percent of Egyptians consider the United States to be an enemy.[41] These results are based on 330,000 people in sixty foreign countries.[42] Given these findings and the clear evidence of waste and corruption and our frightening national debt, it is unreasonable for the United States to expend thirty-eight billion dollars a year in foreign aid. Accordingly, every foreign country currently receiving this aid should be informed in writing that there will be a transitional reduction in the American dollars and military weaponry they currently receive.

Government officials will construct an appropriate schedule for the reductions in foreign aid. Every country should be given twelve months in order for them to make budgetary adjustments. All US foreign aid, both financial and military, should be entirely eliminated within five years from the date of notification. The notifications should specify the exact amounts they will receive in each of the remaining years. When fully implemented, with the elimination of US foreign aid and the closure of diplomatic facilities, the cost savings will be approximately sixty-three billion dollars every year. This is an important starting point as the United States engages in a carefully calibrated transition into a more nuanced position of leadership in a multipolar world. It can be accomplished and should begin immediately. Ending these unhealthy foreign-dependency relationships will have the effect of making these countries stronger and more independent, as they make intelligent use of their abundant natural resources and educate their people to become self-sufficient, productive workers. It will be in America's national interest as well.

Every four years the American Society of Civil Engineers (ASCE) provides a comprehensive assessment of our nation's major infrastructure using an A through F report card format, and citing specific deficiencies, causation, and making recommendations. The ASCE's most recent assessment resulted in a composite rating of D+ for our roads, drinking water, hazardous waste, dams, bridges, rails, et al. It makes little sense for the federal government to send hundreds of billions of taxpayers' money to foreign countries to build roads and airfields when America's infrastructure is degrading to the point of near failure. Readers are reminded that in 2007 an interstate bridge across the Mississippi River collapsed due to a lack of funding. Many of our children are drinking toxic water from school playground fountains.[43]

Today, the United States manages foreign assistance programs in more than one hundred countries around the world through the efforts of over twenty different US government agencies.[44] For readers who think that the proposed reduction in financial aid to foreign countries is too severe, consider the following (see appendix B-1). I selected one country as an example of how the monies are allocated by category. Kenya is the example; readers may choose to examine the comparable data for Egypt, Israel, or any other foreign country. The following data was gleaned from a US government website. There are several other websites that address the matter of foreign aid. Numbers will vary as a function of categories used and funding agency sources. Some programs have multiple sources of funding.

Congressional Budget Justification
Foreign Assistance: Summary Tables
Fiscal Year 2016

KENYA

FY 2016 Request	$630,340,000	p. 13
Global Climate Change	$2,000,000	p. 25
Feed the Future	$42,000,000	p. 31
HIV/AIDS	$456,680,000	pp. 33 and 57

Malaria	$35,000,000	p. 33
Maternal and Child Health	$12,000,000	pp. 33 and 60
Family Planning and Reproductive Health	$27,400,000	pp. 33 and 55
Biodiversity	$3,961,000	p. 37
Education	$5,101,000	pp. 39 and 41
Gender-Based Violence	$4,612,000	p. 51
Nutrition	$7,768.000	p. 62
Tuberculosis	$21,199,000	p. 65
Public Private Partnerships	$10,855,000	p. 69
Science Technology Innovation	$7,820,000	p. 74

(This does not include stateside administrative and evaluation costs, obscure funding sources, or lesser categories: disaster readiness, fish expansion, infrastructure, counterterrorism, etc. Planned United States funding to Kenya in 2017 = $626,367,000.)[45]

The record shows that once federal-aid programs are started, they continue to be funded for years. Consider the emergency plan for AIDS Relief. The US Department of State made the following Diplomacy in Action budget data available for the President's Emergency Plan for AIDS Relief (PEPFAR).

2017 = $5,210,000   2012 = $5,083,000
2016 = $5,217,000   2011 = $5,440,000
2015 = $5,238,000   2010 = $5,574,000
2014 = $4,940,000   2009 = $5,503,000
2013 = $4,726,000   2008 = $5,028,000

Note 1: AIDS funding began in 2004.[46]

Note 2: Readers may be interested in a delineation of FY 2014 Foreign Aid which include monies + military aid. See Appendix B-2 (in maintaining impartiality this list includes the top 21 countries receiving U.S. Aid in descending order of Aid Received. Appendix B-1 list the countries alphabetically.)

CHAPTER THREE

Managing Terrorism and Our National Security

The goal of Islamist terrorists is to kill Americans on American soil. We deny this at our peril. They have killed several thousand Americans already, for the most part, Americans in military positions on foreign soil. But their goal is to kill tens of thousands of American civilians on American soil. Bin Laden told us that in his own words. Make no mistake, they are coming into the United States. Currently, they are 'testing the waters' with pin pricks in Texas and Florida, as they probe our nation's porous borders. This is the new reality, and time is on their side. The enemy is cunning and patient.

The Islamic State is currently perfecting their techniques and strategy, and developing their weapons in Europe. We learned from a laptop computer found in a Syrian safehouse that they are working diligently to weaponize the bubonic plague, to cite just one specific example. Their recent attacks in Paris, London, and Brussels, can be thought of as basic training exercises. Severing the head of a Catholic priest on the altar of a 16th century stone church in Normandy, and running down and crushing two hundred civilians with a rented truck on Bastille Day in Nice may be thought of as the testing of a variety of alternative weapons which are readily available in every American town. It may require a few years, but they are coming. Know that I have no patience or interest in conspiracy theories. My foundation is science and psychology, as well as a reading of history.

The United States has fought the war on terror for the last fifteen years, and we have not defeated the enemy. The facts demonstrate that we are worse off now. Previously, I noted that there are two viable strategies to deal with terrorism. The United States can prosecute a World War II type strategy. With a total governmental and military commitment, within a year the Islamic terrorists in Libya, Iraq, and Syria can be annihilated. We can kill pockets of terrorists in France, Germany, Egypt, Turkey, and Saudi Arabia –– as Iran, the primary state sponsor of global terrorism, secretly perfects nuclear weaponry. There will be collateral civilian destruction. Many Americans will reluctantly endorse this strategy.

I may have tipped my hand in chapter two by delving into the roots of terrorism, and asking why they hate Americans. They have reason. I believe that it is in America's best interest to embark on a different viable strategy of 'managing terrorism'. This is not a capitulation. We will win the war on terror. It will take longer, but it will be long-lasting. It will also spare several thousand lives. Converting the U.S. embassies in Africa and the Middle East into virtual embassies, followed by the closing of military bases and returning our troops stateside is an initial step. Difficult as it will be (many will say cruel), cutting off all foreign economic and military aid to foreign countries will benefit Americans immediately. One hundred billion dollars each year can be invested in complete border security with Canada and Mexico, and jumpstart an enhanced intelligence service.

Disadvantaged populations will learn to meet their needs. It will be difficult. With motivation and determination men flew to the moon, planted a flag, and returned safely to earth. Four thousand years ago, man constructed magnificient architectural structures in the desert. Many of these pyramids are still looked upon with wonderment at what man can accomplish.

Natural resources on the African continent are abundant. Dams and roads can be built. Land can be cultivated and farms developed. Streams, lakes, and rivers can be repopulated. Livestock can be domesticated. Minerals, precious stones and metals, and timber can be marketed worldwide. Children can be educated and develop an appreciation for work, self determination, and destiny control.

Appreciate what the people in Israel did with their barren desert territory, as they fended off hostile neighbors on every border. These achievements can be replicated, and Israel will be among the first to step up and share their knowledge and technology if foreign leaders request this form of assistance. The recipients will be made stronger in the process which will not happen if there is a continuous flow of monies from the West. We see clear evidence of this human dynamic in the United States. Have we enabled our Native Americans to achieve self-determination and self-sufficiency over the last two hundred years! Drive onto their reservations, visit with these good people, and you will answer the question.

The 9/11 attacks made the war on terror a corollary of American foreign policy, which propelled our military into Afghanistan and, thereafter, into Iraq, Libya, Yemen, and Syria. Terrorism can be likened to cancer in that there is no cure, and it spreads like cancer. But cancer is being managed effectively, and terrorism can also be managed effectively. It must be managed at home and abroad simultaneously. Stateside, our borders with Canada and Mexico are not secure. US immigration laws and regulations are outdated and not consistently enforced. Security at our airports and seaports needs to be hardened. And we need to develop a strategy for the early identification of homegrown terrorists. Specific recommendations regarding stateside security will be detailed in the national security section of this chapter.

Managing terrorism abroad will require a radical change in current military strategy. By attacking terrorists abroad, we are effectively creating more terrorists than we are killing. This is a no-win strategy. We need to improve the working relationship between our military and intelligence communities. We need to learn more from past mistakes.

John Miller is a well-known former journalist and deputy commissioner of Intelligence and Counterterrorism for the New York City Police Department. What is less well-known is that between the World Trade Center attack in 1993 and the WTC attack on September 11, 2001, Miller met with Osama Bin Laden in Afghanistan in May 1998. He asked Bin Laden, "Why would a man of your wealth, from a powerful Saudi family, have gone to Afghanistan to live in trenches and fight the Russian invaders?" Osama replied, "It is hard for one to understand if the person does not understand Islam. Our battle with Americans is larger than our battle with the Russians. The American imposes himself on everyone. We are sure of our victory against Americans. Everywhere Americans went where Muslims lived, all they did was kill our children and occupy Muslim land. In Iraq, the American-led sanctions resulted in the deaths of more than one million Iraqi children. We believe that the biggest thieves in the world and the biggest terrorists are the Americans. The only way for us to fend off these assaults is to use similar means."[47] Readers can view YouTube and hear Bin Laden speaking with Miller.

Not only did US intelligence fail to prevent 9/11, it took a decade to find and kill Bin Laden. The United States could have captured him much sooner. Osama's large compound was located one mile from the Pakistan Military Academy in Abbottabad, which is a suburb where many retired military officers, as well as instructors from the academy, live. The academy is similar in function to West Point and provides training to the officers of the Pakistan Army.[48] It is inconceivable to this writer that with more than a thousand military students, faculty, and families within reasonable proximity to the compound, they would be unaware of the identity of the inhabitants. The United States gives the Pakistanis a billion dollars each year. Their military and intelligence personnel know their American counterparts. There is ongoing dialogue between intelligence officers in the United States and in Pakistan. None of these officers signaled an alarm upon hearing the muffled sounds from the gigantic helicopters landing within the compound? Americans are led to believe that Pakistani military personnel and their families (and pet dogs) did not hear the US attack helicopters crash-landing on the rooftop of Bin Laden's compound, the repeating rounds of artillery fire, or the explosives used to breath the hardened metal doors?

Pakistan has been accepting billions of American dollars for years as they have been playing both sides of the street. The Pakistani government has been providing safe harbor to the Taliban going at least back to the Battle of Tora Bora in December of 2001 when Bin Laden escaped into the tribal areas of Pakistan. It is widely believed that a Pakistan Air Force helicopter airlifted Bin Laden from Tora Bora into a safe haven in Pakistan.

The United States has had difficulty identifying terrorists within our borders. In 2009, a mass shooting took place in Fort Hood, Texas. Nidal Hasan, a US Army major and medical psychiatrist, fatally shot thirteen people and wounded thirty others.[49] Hasan had e-mailed a top al-Qaeda recruiter in Yemen eighteen times and had a history of making jihadist utterances. He also carried business cards with SOA (Soldier of Allah) printed on them.[50] Dr. Hassan is currently living in the Disciplinary Barracks at Fort Leavenworth, where he recently wrote a letter to Abu Bakr Baghdadi, requesting citizenship with the militant Islamic State. We feed, clothe, shelter, and meet his religious and health requirements.

In 2015, American-led air strikes are estimated to have killed more than twenty thousand Islamic State fighters.[51] The former chairman of the Joint Chiefs of Staff, General Martin Dempsey, stated that ISIS cannot be defeated militarily. "ISIS will only truly be defeated when it is rejected by the 20 million disenfranchised Sunni that happen to reside between Damascus and Baghdad."[52]

Colonel Gulmurod Khalimov, a US-trained commander resurfaced in an Islamic State video and promised to bring jihad to his native Tajikistan, as well as to the Americans who trained him. "I was in America three times," Col. Khalimov said in the video. "I saw how you train fighters so they can kill Muslims."[53] This hatred is deep and increasingly widespread.

Wherever the United States has left its footprint, living conditions are much worse now. Yemen is battling extremism on several fronts after the overthrow of their government in 2012. Afghanistan is struggling to contain a resurgent Taliban. US troops have been on the ground there for fifteen years! We should have known better. The Soviet Union's military troops were fighting in Afghanistan from 1979 until 1989 and left the country in frustration, with 14,453 Soviet troops killed and 53,753 wounded. Civilian death estimates vary from 850,000 to 1,500,000, and between five to ten million Afghans fled to Pakistan and India.[54]

The United States also had a civilian project in Afghanistan from 1954 through 1978. We should have learned a great deal about their tribal conflicts and corrupt leadership as we developed an educational program for the country. We published seventy-five textbooks in Dari and Pashto. A colleague of mine, Professor Butts, stated, "So anything to spread American influence in Afghanistan was a contribution to our efforts in the Cold War . . . Yes, democratic nation-building must be the goal of any long-range assistance by the U.S.A. to Afghanistan . . . That was the implied goal of the Teachers College's Afghan Project in the middle of the 20th century, but now it must be the pervasive and explicit goal of the 21st century."[55] Butts ran the Afghan Project from 1955 to 1975. Teachers College also ran similar programs in Africa, Asia, and Latin America.[56] Sixty years of American involvement in Afghanistan, and the results are self-evident. Security has been deteriorating since US force levels dropped from a high of one hundred thousand in 2011 to now under ten thousand.[57] It is this author's studied judgment that the United States has inadvertently planted the seeds of terrorism by bombing Afghanistan, Iraq, Syria, and other countries. These seeds are now sprouting in acts of terrorism targeting Americans and will continue to do so.

In Iraq, how many times does the US military have to take back Fallujah? Did we save Ramadi or destroy Ramadi? Many believe that Iraqi Muslims had a better life under the strong long rule of Saddam Hussein. We need to think and have empathy for how Muslims feel when they walk through bombed neighborhoods and see homes, schools, and mosques reduced to rubble. Americans need to see through their eyes and feel what they feel. Then we will begin to understand the roots of terrorism.

In Libya, Muammar Gaddafi effectively ruled from 1969 until he was killed in 2011. With ISIS presently eyeing the rich oil-production potential, one can expect further turmoil. At stake are Libya's forty-seven billion barrels of crude oil reserves, the largest in Africa and the source of virtually all of the country's wealth. Concerned about easy access to their border, the European Union is pressing the United States to lead a coalition of military forces to expel ISIS. Libya has become a failed state. Boko Haram recently declared its allegiance to the Islamic State. When Libya falls, it may have a domino effect on the African continent. The United States has a drone base in Niger and is constructing a larger drone base in Cameroon. One can anticipate death and destruction in African villages. The United States needs to understand that throwing out strong leaders merely opens the doors for the kind of chaos that sucks in American troops and creates problems that turn out to be worse than the ones that the United States was trying to solve.

Recently, Senator Cruz advocated carpet bombing ISIS. He stated, "We will carpet bomb them into oblivion, and I don't know if sand can glow in the dark, but we're going to find out." Cruz is reminded of the shock and awe rained upon Baghdad. According to Brian Whitaker, "To some in the Arab and Muslim countries, shock and awe is terrorism by another name."[58]

Yet the Pentagon's budget request for 2017 of $583 billion includes $1.8 billion to procure forty-five thousand bombs and rockets.[59] In a manner of thinking, this can be likened to planting forty-five thousand terrorist seeds and will result in more American troops driving over IEDs as they fight terrorists in foreign countries. The United States will never be able to bomb its way free of terrorism. The Pentagon ought to acknowledge the reality and save the lives of thousands of Muslims and Americans.

President Obama is currently on his fourth secretary of defense. Yet there is little evidence of changed thinking. Nothing changes, and we don't learn from past mistakes. Most readers are familiar with Black Hawk Down in Somalia where our dead crew members were dragged through the streets of Mogadishu in 1993. In 2006, the United States paid Somali warlords to do our bidding in the Second Battle of Mogadishu.[60] In 2013, the US SEAL team 6 launched a daring nighttime raid on an al-Shabaab safe house in Somalia, which did not go well.[61] In 2016, a US air strike using drones and jets killed more people (150) in one day than during the previous nine years of US attacks in Somalia.[62] The *Pittsburgh Post-Gazette* summed it up by stating that the biggest concern for Americans is that such a major attack on al-Shabaab militants risks provoking a revenge assault on the United States. It would be foolish for the United States to imagine that such an attack could not occur. So why is the United States still involved in an expensive, unsuccessful effort in Somalia? This news item makes my point that our war on terror is creating more terror, and it is coming inside the United States.

It should be noted that these incursions in Somalia have been supported by both Republican and Democratic administrations. George H.W. Bush sent American troops into Somalia in what was largely a humanitarian mission. Bill Clinton followed with his 'nation building' effort in Somalia.

The most lethal attacks by radical Muslims on American soil have been homegrown like Fort Hood and the Boston Marathon. In both cases, the attackers seem to have been driven by the perception that the United States is at war with Islam.[63] As the US drone bombs ISIS abroad, more individuals within the United

States will see these as acts against Islam and conduct terror strikes on American civilians.

The US military continues to rain death and destruction on African people. The Pentagon has sent three hundred troops to Cameroon to fight the Islamist terrorists of Boko Haram in neighboring Nigeria, and it's an open secret that the United States operates a drone base in Garowa in northern Cameroon. A recent US air strike in Libya killed an Islamic State leader and forty-eight terrorist comrades, and the Pentagon is reported to be drawing up plans for a broader air campaign in Libya. In 2013, the United States set up a drone base in Niger, which has borders with Nigeria, Algeria, Mali, and Libya. Altogether, the United States operates surveillance flights from about twelve small sites in Africa. The risk is that the United States will keep playing catch-up against a threat growing faster than we can destroy or even contain.[64]

Muslims are not America's enemies. However, radical jihadist seeds can sprout anywhere, even in America. We must understand and prepare for this eventuality. Syrian rebels found a laptop in an ISIS hideout that contained extensive information on how to construct biological weapons, how to weaponize the bubonic plague, and how to test the weaponized disease safely before it is used in a terrorist attack.[65]

Magnus Ranstorp, who previously testified before the 9/11 Commission, is the research director of the Center for Asymmetric Threat Studies in Sweden. Relative to the laptop, he recently stated, "To produce quite scary weapons is certainly within the Islamic State's capabilities."[66] We know that there are other San Bernardino–like extremists working, praying, and studying in America. A biological weapon concealed in a backpack or briefcase has the potential to kill thousands of people in an American city. ISIS can inspire believers to attack stateside. Extremists in

American cities read the gory details on the Internet. We must never forget that it was local Timothy McVeigh who killed 168 people in Oklahoma City, Eric Rudolph detonated the Olympic Park bomb in Atlanta, and the Tsarnaev brothers at the Boston Marathon. This is not idle speculation. Rather it is a tragic reality.

Americans need to also anticipate other threat sources. The National Alliance on Mental Illness reports that ten million adults experience a serious mental illness each year. Every American town is home to individuals with schizoid personalities, others suffer with manic depression, and a huge range of anxiety disorders. These individuals are vulnerable, and when stimulated by spectacular media reports may feel themselves in a psychotic attack episode. There will be attacks that are only in this bizarre manner related to terrorism. We need to anticipate lone wolf attacks in shopping malls, schools, at athletic events, and other public gatherings. People need to understand that while the threat is real, they ought not abandon their freedom of movement or alter their lifestyle. Within fifty states, the probability of any one individual being victimized is exceedingly low. Continue enjoying life with reason and caution. There is no remedy on the horizon. There is simply no way to stop these 'low tech' attacks. In time, they will waste away. In the meantime, we can ameliorate and manage.

The United States can best manage terrorism by discontinuing the bombing in Somalia and the Middle East. Redeploy these troops stateside to patrol our Canadian border while the security wall is completed on our Southern border. It is exceedingly difficult to guard against the lone-wolf attacker, as we have seen. But we can do a lot better. In the "Available Health Care" section of chapter 5, a plan will be put forth that will significantly enhance our ability to pre-identify potential terrorists at the local community level. It is easy to observe the person who sits alone in the cafeteria or who utters rambling, radicalized thoughts in the workplace, but we can do much more. By employing mental health specialists in local health care centers who are trained to see with a third eye, counselors have the ability to transpose themselves into the thinking, feeling, and acting of another person and so structure the world as he or she does.[67] This is best accomplished in our local communities where everyone knows a little bit about other locals.

Stateside terrorists will seek to target our infrastructure. Local enforcement agencies need to work in concert with the Department of Homeland Security and the FBI with a focus on hardening vulnerable facilities. The water reservoirs of every metropolitan area need to be secured, and this is presently not happening. Ted Koppel addresses in detail his concern about the threat to our power grid. He asserts that an attack on our power grid is very likely but that the United States has no plan for that eventuality.[68] The United States must anticipate that ISIS-inspired terrorists will attempt to target our water and power facilities. Many major cities have protective strategies in place, but every American deserves the comfort of this protection. Rush wrote, "Americans must accept the fact that there's nothing they can do to rid the whole world of mean people and evil behavior. The U.S. has a big enough job simply watching out for its own national interests."[69] The government mantra "We're fighting them overseas, so we don't have to fight them at home" became outmoded with the end of WWII. When the US military exits the Middle East, the world will witness Arab states stepping in to stabilize regional conditions. And if desirable, from an Arab perspective, the United Nations can be engaged to assume a peacekeeping role.

A decade after the nation's sixteen spy agencies were consolidated under the Office of the Director of National Intelligence, security experts are expressing concerns about interagency rivalries and questioning whether the intelligence community is prepared to deal with domestic and foreign threats.[70] The United States' intelligence community is the strongest government body to protect the homeland. They are tasked with the enormous responsibility of maintaining our nation's security. They are engaged in an ongoing threat assessment of enemies who are continuously morphing and present a complex array of sophisticated threats. They deserve all the resources required to properly execute their mission. Regarding concern about interagency coordination and rivalries, we should have confidence in the National Intelligence Coordination Center and the Joint Worldwide Intelligence Communication System. Our intelligence leaders must continue their relationships of mutual respect and cooperation with the BND in Germany, the MI5 in the UK, and the Mossad in Israel.

Oversight of our intelligence agencies is shared by the Permanent Select Committee on Intelligence in the House and the Senate Select Committee on Intelligence. Senate and House reports that accompanied the 2014 Consolidated Appropriations Act included provision for the Government Accountability Office (GAO) to review the implementation of the National Cybersecurity Protection System (NCPS). The GAO report detailed nine recommendations to be undertaken by the Department of Homeland Security to enhance NCPS's capabilities for meeting its objectives. DHS concurred with all nine recommendations.[71]

The United States has not been staying ahead of cyber attacks in several important areas. Recently, the Federal Reserve Bank of New York uncovered bogus payment orders, copies of which were reviewed by the Wall Street Journal, that show how cyber thieves stole $81 million from Bangladesh's account at the New York Fed. During the same timeframe, the journal reported that two websites, the Guccifer 2.0 WordPress and DCLeaks.com, both of which are believed by computer experts to have direct ties to Russian intelligence services, have leaked sensitive political and government information to the media. Guccifer 2.0 posted a spreadsheet containing the personal cell phone numbers and email addresses of close to 200 current and former House of Representative Democrats and their senior staff members. By having access to cell phone numbers and email addresses, spies and hackers can likely intercept communications to and from these lawmakers, particularly those on sensitive committees that oversee U.S. intelligence and military operations.

DCLeaks.com previously published the content of emails and records connected to the Democratic Party, as well as those of Air Force General Philip Breedlove, the former supreme commander of the North Atlantic Treaty Organization (NATO). Cyber security firms that have scrutinized these hacks have pointed to evidence that show that the breaches came from two well-known cyber espionage groups with suspected links to the Russian government.

These cyber attacks strike at the core of America's government. At what point do they reach the threat level. At what point do they constitute acts of war. At this time, the government does not have definitive answers. The U.S. is falling behind our adversaries. The Federal Reserve Bank of New York is not secure. Congressional communications are not secure. It may well be that World War III will be fought in cyberspace, and the United States is not adequately prepared. The U.S. Cyber Command must be fully funded.

US intelligence agencies must be continuously on the alert for efforts to compromise not only our power and water facilities but our finance and banking structure as well.[72] Cyberattackers compromised the US Department of Energy computer system 159 times. The National Nuclear Security Administration responsible for securing the nation's nuclear weapons stockpile experienced nineteen successful attacks.[73] Presently, cyberdefense efforts are being enhanced by work of the US Cyber Command and by the National Defense University. Likewise, the Defense Department has made the data available in its Automated Biometric Identification System to the FBI and DHS.[74]

Currently, the US Cyber Command is struggling to fight cyberwarfare with one arm tied behind its back because the United States has no policy on what type and level of cyberattack constitutes an act of war against America. At a February 9, 2016, Senate Armed Services Committee hearing, General Vincent Stewart (director of the Defense Intelligence Agency) testified, "If the military had a much fuller definition of the range of acts that occur in cyberspace and then start thinking about the threshold where an attack is catastrophic enough or destructive enough that we define it as an act of war. I think that would be very helpful." In May, Senator Rounds of South Dakota introduced the Cyber Act of War Act of 2016, which will require the administration to define what constitutes an act of war in cyberspace and consider the ways in which the effects of a cyberattack may be equivalent to the effects of an attack using conventional weapons. This strategic clarity is long overdue, and the Cyber Act of War Act of 2016 should be voted into law now.

While fighting on these fronts, our intelligence agencies are struggling to balance civil liberties and privacy rights with their need to gather big data and monitor subjects that are gleaned from the data. Americans need to appreciate that they enjoy these rights and freedoms because of the work being done by these agencies to protect our national security. Apple Corporation has thus far resisted the FBI's request for technical assistance with unlocking the smartphone used by the San Bernardino murderers.

The Foreign Intelligence Surveillance Act has been dumbed down with onerous requirements to secure authorizing court orders. Legal and bureaucratic impediments to surveillance should be removed, including the Presidential Policy Directive 28, which bestows privacy rights to foreigners and imposes burdensome requirements to justify data collection. This Directive 28 should be rescinded.

Pompeo and Rivkin argue that reasonable, warrantless searches are compatible with the Fourth Amendment. So are searches of data shared with third parties, such as social media posts that are a valuable surveillance window, since people undergoing radicalization are prone to showcase their zealotry online.[75] We need to continue our efforts to engage key components in the private sector. Initial efforts with Google, Microsoft, Apple, and Facebook have not gone well. However, it is encouraging to learn that Twitter suspended 125,000 accounts associated with the Islamic State that had maintained an expansive Twitter presence for its propaganda and recruiting efforts. The social media company is relying on a mix of human judgment and technology, developing teams of specialists that comb through thousands of suspect accounts.[76]

What our intelligence agencies ought not to be doing is monitoring the personal phone conversations of government leaders in friendly nations. There is compelling evidence that Chancellor Merkel's phone was tapped. Germany's Federal Intelligence Service (BND) evaluated the evidence and concluded that there was sufficient information to confront the Obama administration.[77] The next president should issue a directive to the US intelligence community to discontinue this practice. There should also be an executive order that limits the use of drones by the CIA to data collection and also places a complete ban on the CIA's use of weaponized drones. This would not affect the military use of drones.

The most immediate threat to our nation's national security is the lack of secure borders and inadequate immigration policies and procedures. The great melting pot that served America so well in the past is not viable in an age of terror. We need to learn from what we observe currently happening in the European Union. Great nations demonstrating their humanitarian concern and their generosity are being overwhelmed by the myriad of problems associated with providing for and integrating vast waves of immigration. There is evidence that radical extremists have blended in with over a million refugees and made their way into Germany, France, Spain, and Italy. Borders must be controlled. This is simply common sense.

The Department of Homeland Security includes the agency Immigration Control Enforcement (ICE). Their mission is to identify, arrest, and remove aliens who present a danger to our national security or a risk to public safety. ICE has twenty thousand employees in more than four hundred offices in the United States and in forty-eight foreign countries.[78] Their Enforcement and Removal Operation (ERO) unit enforces our immigration laws. ERO transports removable aliens from point to point, manages aliens in custody or in an alternative detention program, provides access to legal resources and representatives of advocacy groups. This writer recommends the discontinuation of referral to advocacy groups.

Examining the FY 2008–2015 ICE removals data, it can be observed that they removed approximately 2,878,670 individuals of whom about 50 percent were convicted criminals.[79] It is noted that the number of removals has declined as follows: 2012 = 409,849 removals, 2013 = 368,644, 2014 = 315,943, and 2015 =

235,413.[80] These numbers demonstrate a porous border. All illegal immigrants with a criminal conviction should be immediately deported without being given access to legal counsel or referral to an advocacy group. ICE has reported that 124 illegal immigrants released from jail by the Obama administration since 2010 have been subsequently charged with murder. ICE released 30,558 criminal aliens who had been convicted of 92,347 crimes in 2014, and only 3 percent has been deported. This list does not include those released by over 300 so-called "sanctuary cities."[81] I recommend that every sanctuary city should be denied federal funds. We need to seek the abolishment of all state and local sanctuary laws and policies.

Given my cursory review of the four hundred federal statutes that ICE is responsible for enforcing, I believe that most of these laws and regulations should have been stricken from the books years ago. These illegals, particularly convicted criminals, have too many rights and privileges. The reader is reminded that in 2015, thirty-one-year-old Kate Steinle was killed by an undocumented Mexican immigrant who had seven prior felony convictions and had been deported five times back into Mexico. Sanctuary cities are in violation of the Illegal Immigration Reform and Immigrant Responsibility Act of 1996. These city policies impede the ability of law enforcement officers to identify illegal aliens and process them for deportation.

The federal government should freeze immigration for an indefinite period of time, with provision for extreme-hardship visas in a very limited number of cases.

The US Army Corps of Engineers (USACE) is a federal agency under the Department of Defense. It consists of thirty-seven thousand civilian and military personnel, making it one of the world's largest engineering, design, and construction management agencies. It is primarily funded by the American taxpayers. USACE provides technical and construction support to more than 130 countries worldwide.[82] The corps also did reimbursable work in Iran, Jordan, Kuwait, and Libya.[83] I recommend that the US Army Corps of Engineers be directed to construct a security barrier wall along the entire US side of the Mexican border. The wall should be impenetrable and untunnelable and be equipped with state-of-the-art imaging and signaling instruments.

Further, by presidential order, the US Border Patrol should be directed to order (in English and Spanish) any individual attempting to cross the border into the United States to stop and reverse direction, with agents having the authorization to shoot anyone who does not obey the command.[84]

Canada and the United States have the world's largest shared border. There are one hundred nineteen official border crossings. Approximately, twenty-eight thousand trucks cross the border each day, one hundred forty thousand cars, and three hundred thousand people each day.[85] This last number includes workers, tourists, and some who come to harm Americans. The Government Accountability Office (GAO) report concluded that the risk of terrorist activity is high on the Northern border and that only thirty-two of the almost four thousand miles of the US-Canadian border have reached an acceptable level of control in 2010.

Back then, the ICE director John Morton testified before the judiciary subcommittee on Immigration, Refugees, and Border Security, stating, "We removed 47,000 illegal aliens from the Northern border region, roughly half of whom are criminal offenders."[86] Alongside Morton was Alan Bersin, commissioner of US Customs and Border Control Protection (CBP), who testified that CBP interdicts around forty thousand pounds of illegal drugs each year, at and between points of entry along the Northern border, and that the United States will begin deploying military-grade radar along the Northern border in an effort to thwart low-flying aircraft used to smuggle narcotics into the United States."[87] This was very troubling sworn testimony by the highest-ranking officials in US border control and protection.

To wit, the United States has more than 3,500 miles of unprotected border, captured forty-seven thousand illegal aliens in one year, and seizes forty thousand pounds of illegal drugs each year. This is a huge terrorist threat, and it is being exploited. The United States seized forty thousand pounds, which suggests that an additional one hundred thousand–plus pounds might have passed into the United States. Therefore, it is a reasonable assumption that a dozen terrorists also passed into the United States. Evidence of this condition is beginning to mount. Bedard reported, "The nexus between known or suspected terrorists in eastern Canada and the northern parts of the United States represents a significant national security threat . . . from a 100 page report by the Senate Homeland Security and Governmental Affairs Committee." It comes at a time when Canada is preparing to settle twenty-five thousand Syrian refugees by March 2016.

The Senate report continues, "If someone gets into Canada, they most likely will be able to enter the United States . . . And for thousands of miles of border, for most there is only a six plus inch ditch and forest to stop them. There is no fencing on the northern border . . . Communities in Minneapolis, Minnesota and Rochester, New York (two states which are contiguous with Ontario and Quebec) have already experienced terrorist threats. On November 26, 2014, two men in Minneapolis were charged with recruiting and conspiring to provide support to ISIL. Likewise, on September 17, 2014, a man in Rochester NY was arrested on similar charges after the FBI provided evidence showing that he attempted to recruit fighters and funds for ISIL."[88] This border threat is very serious, more so than incidents on our Southern border.

The US border with Mexico is half as long as our border with Canada. Yet we have approximately six thousand border-patrol agents on the Northern border and eighteen thousand protective agents on the Southern border.[89] It is recommended that the United States deploy twenty thousand agents on the Canadian border and reduce to ten thousand the number of agents on the Mexican border.

Ninety-three percent of Canadian energy exports go to the United States. The Obama administration strained the American-Canadian energy trade relationship by rejecting TransCanada's permit for the Keystone XL Pipeline. The US State Department had already concluded that the project was environmentally safe. With the world's longest land border and common Western values, the United States and Canada should work together in their efforts to combat terrorism.[90] In the 2010 Joint Border Threat and Risk Assessment, US and Canadian border officials emphasized that terrorism in one country is a national security threat to the other.

We need to secure our Northern border because Canada does use different criteria in granting immigrant visas. This is just one of several reasons why the United States must tighten up its own visa program.

Senator Richard Burr, chairman of the Senate Intelligence Committee, was recently quoted as stating that terrorists traveling from Europe without a visa pose a bigger threat to US security than refugees from Syria.[91] However, it is not either-or; we need to block all the threats to US security. The US Visa Waiver Program was significantly hardened with the enactment of Visa Waiver

Program Improvement and Terrorist Prevention Act of 2015, which was signed into law on December 18, 2015.[92]

However, the Diversity Immigrant Visa, commonly referred to as the Green Card Lottery, is fraught with security issues. In short, each year, fifty thousand permanent resident visas are given away to citizens of countries with low immigration rates into the United States through a lottery process. This is a random-selection process that enables fifty thousand people to receive permanent resident visas through the Green Card lottery. These individuals from foreign countries can live and work permanently in the United States and bring a spouse and unmarried children under the age of twenty-one with them.[93] It is my studied judgment that the Diversity Visa Program is outmoded and a threat to America's national security. Accordingly, this unfair and dangerous lottery program should be abolished by Congress, immediately. It is important to recognize that the standard employment-based green card programs (EB1, EB2, and EB3) are in our nation's interest. They are reasonable, secure, and desirable. While they may be ripe for 2017 tweaking, these programs should remain in place.

It is imperative that the foregoing recommendations be implemented as quickly as is reasonable. Once US physical borders have been secured and our immigration statutes have been updated with new restrictions and requirements and border-patrol agents are directed to enforce all immigration laws and regulations, the freeze on immigration should be lifted. No applicant should be denied access on the basis of race, religion, or country of origin. Each must be thoroughly vetted by a Department of Homeland Security agency. Those who are evaluated to be acceptable will be required to submit to fingerprinting and facial-recognition protocols and have appropriate DNA specimens collected. If there is provision for a risk category, these individuals will be required to give permission to have a tracking chip implanted, which, if removed or otherwise deactivated, will signal an alert in the Immigration Control Enforcement's unit of responsibility and a warrant for arrest issued. They should be expeditiously deported.

Eventually, the United States will have to take some action regarding the 11.4 million undocumented immigrants presently living in the United States. Recent debates were chock-full of plans; most were unrealistic. For example, candidates Trump and Cruz state that they would deport them all. Trump would bring nearly half of them back through the regular immigration procedure based on existing laws and regulations. A study released in March 2016 found that the federal government would need to spend between four hundred billion dollars and six hundred billion dollars just to deport the undocumented.[94] Readers are reminded that each immigrant would have to be apprehended and detained while they await due process, being moved through the courts and then transported to their home countries. Pew reports that only about half are actually from Mexico. The rest come from Central America (15.2 percent), Asia (12.4 percent), South America (6.3 percent), and the remaining 18.5 percent are from Europe, the Caribbean, the Middle East, Africa, and elsewhere.[95] The physical removal effort would demand, on average, eighty-four buses and forty-seven chartered flights every day for two years.[96] This mass deportation would be impractical, expensive, and probably ineffective. Most undocumented individuals are of good character and obey the law. Some do not. According to the AAA Foundation for Traffic Safety, 8,400 people on average die each year in crash with unlicensed drivers. Approximately half are the victims of illegal immigrants. These individuals must be deported and never permitted to re-enter the United States.

It has previously been noted that the overwhelming majority of Muslims, both here and abroad, are honest, nonviolent, hardworking people. I believe that our 11.4 million unauthorized immigrants can be similarly characterized. I urge that they be placed on a safe and speedy track to American citizenship. We need to free these people from living in the shadows, wondering if a stranger who knocks on their door for directions may take them into custody. My recommendation is reasonable, humane, and in our national interest. It is good for them, good for the economy, and good for America.

CHAPTER FOUR

Resetting Foreign Policy and Refocusing the Military

In the preceding chapters, the groundwork was laid for rethinking American foreign policy and the best use of our military forces. Recommendations were made to reduce the US global footprint by closing selected diplomatic facilities and to begin the disengagement of military forces in Africa and the Middle East. It was further proposed that the United States eliminate all foreign aid, both financial and military weaponry.

We are living in an increasingly dangerous world. The United States is being perceived differently in terms of its leadership role. In 2012, President Obama stated "we have been very clear to the Assad regime that a red line for us is if we start seeing chemical weapons being utilized in Syria.... and we have communicated in no uncertain terms with every player in the region that that is a red line for us and that there would be serious consequences if we start seeing movement on the chemical weapons front or the use of chemical weapons." In August 2013, the Syrian military attacked rebel-controlled areas of Damascus suburbs with chemical weapons, killing nearly 1,500 civilians including more than 400 children. As the world knows, there were no consequences.

On August 16, 2016, the Wall Street Journal reported that Russia launched airstrikes against targets in Syria from an airbase in Iran. The bombings are a sign of a new coordination between Moscow and Tehran to support President Assad, and an indication that the United States has fallen short in its efforts to draw Russia away from a close military alliance with Iran. It is entirely likely that Russia will transfer nuclear capability to Iran. Russia has lost respect for the United States as a world power. Israel feels betrayed because of the reckless manner in which the United States negotiated the nuclear deal with Iran, the world's leading sponsor of terrorism. Many of our European allies have begun to resent us. Some question our resolve. Others are angry that our NSA compromised their private telephonic communications. The United States has made conditions worse wherever we involved our military in Africa and the Middle East. It is timely to rethink our role in the world. There are alternatives.

Our U.S. foreign policy has far too long been based on the premise that if we contain the spread of Communism and preserve world order around the globe, America would remain the leader of the world, and Americans will be secure and prosper. This has proven by bitter experience not to be the case, and the costs have been prohibitive in terms of both blood and money. In reality, there will always be violent internal conflicts, as well as social, political, and religious upheavals around the world. The United States can no longer afford to maintain our military forces on every continent; protect European nations against largely self-inflicted wounds; feed, protect, and shelter people across the globe. The U.S. is not the answer to the world's problems. At best, these never ending worldwide issues can be managed. Conflicted and unstable states are best managed by countries in the region that understand the history, culture, tribal groupings, and religious rivalries.... countries that have a direct vested interest in the state of affairs.

A group of regional middle powers must emerge to manage disorder in their area. Absent direct U.S. involvement, this will occur naturally and be infinitely more effective. The United States has not adequately understood the genesis of most of the foreign regional conflicts that we have attempted to ameliorate, and have all too frequently left conditions worse than we found them. In Iraq, Syria, Libya, and Afghanistan our trepidation and qualms about escalation limited our interventions at the point where the pursuit of success would have meant an enlarged military engagement and violence to the people we were trying to protect. The U.S. has failed in resolving many disputes which are local, bitter, longstanding, and have little to do with America even in the increasingly global nature of the 21st century. We have lost the war against forces of oppression and chaos in foreign lands. There are alternatives.

United States hegemony began with the Marshall Plan (European Recovery Program), which President Truman signed into law in 1948. The $130 billion (current dollars) in economic support helped rebuild Western Europe in the aftermath of WWII. The United States assumed major responsibility for maintaining global security. Our role as hegemon expanded over the years, as the United States wielded its economic and military power around the world and soon controlled the air and sea, giving us the unique ability to strike anywhere on the globe. Subsequently, domestic prosperity within the US borders gave us the position of leadership in the international economy.

Times have changed. During the past two decades, Americans have come to the realization that hegemony is both expensive and provocative. In FY 2015, Pentagon-related spending was $598 billion.[97] The United States has depleted its financial resources patrolling the skies and keeping the shipping lanes open for international trade, stabilizing failing states, and promoting democracy around the world. The recent collapse in our economy has further reduced our position of dominance around the globe, as we have asked secondary powers to share more of the cost of maintaining US military forces in their countries. We have begun to push them to accept more responsibility for maintaining a stable world order. But there has been pushback. Germany, France, Turkey, and even the Saudis are stepping away from US control, suggesting that they may welcome a leveling of world power and dominance. Already, King Salman has put a coalition of Arab states' troops into Yemen to stabilize it and is planning with Turkey to send troops into Syria.

The American electorate has also become dissatisfied with our costly role as the leader of the world while ignoring deteriorating living conditions here at home. We see evidence of this attitudinal change reflected in the early voting patterns in elections for a new administration. Americans are demanding a radical change in direction, suggesting that its government shift its emphasis from worldwide priorities to domestic priorities. Americans are not unaware of the increase in anti-American sentiment abroad, especially in Muslim countries. They witness the decline of US prestige in Europe. They see that our ally, Israel, no longer trusts American leadership.

By 2025, the United States will find itself as just one of a number of important actors on the world stage.[98] This report was produced by the Office of the Director of National Intelligence (ODNI), which is a coalition of America's top seventeen agencies that gather and analyze intelligence necessary to conduct foreign relations.[99] They issued their first Global Trends report in 1997. Their 2008 assessment revealed that the whole international system as constructed after WWII will be revolutionized. New powers will bring new stakes and rules and predicted an unprecedented transfer of wealth from West to East. We do see evidence of these prognostications.

In their 2012 report (Global Trends 2030), they indicated that China would overtake the United States as a global power around 2030 or 2040. Looks like it may be closer to 2040, as China's economy has hit a speed bump. They wrote that middle-class consumption in China and India will grow dramatically, overtaking the West's middle class, and that the economic rise of Asian giants India and China is likely to have drastic implications for the world, the balance of power, and America's place in it.[100] The Global Trends 2035 report will be issued in December 2016, after the presidential election. My expectation is that it will predict the end of American hegemony and the continued rise of a multipolar world. The gathering evidence is undeniable. We are no longer living in a unipolar world. Historically, every great nation eventually declined. The United States is in its final stage of world leadership, which is not a negative for America or the world. The only way to reverse the trend will be through our military power, and that will have catastrophic consequences for civilization.

There is no good reason to even attempt to reverse the trend into a multipolar world. However, it is in our national interest to control our own national destiny. We ought not to allow our future to be defined by secondary powers. We need to develop a smart strategy that combines both our hard and soft power resources. I have already indicated the best use of our military power. It is clear that economic, political, social, and diplomatic powers are becoming more important than military power in the international system. The United States can still maintain a strong position of influence in the world. We must join with other world leaders in maintaining global order and stability through peaceful strategies. The United States must not be goaded into the use of American military forces. It is imperative that the United States engage in a carefully calculated and voluntary withdrawal from its role of global dominance as the superpower leader of the world. Know that the world will not implode without our global military involvement and will not revert to the dark period of the 1930s. On the contrary, shared leadership will guarantee global stability. We need to cultivate Russia as an ally and encourage the participation of India, Saudi Arabia, and China to join the stage of world leaders in maintaining global order and stability.

It should be noted that there are others who see the world differently. For example, Richard Haass has been president of the influential Council on Foreign Relations since 2003, and has stated that the consequences of a lasting American retreat from the world would be dire.... and that we cannot become a giant gated community. Pat Buchanan responds better than I when he writes, "No it was not isolationists who failed America. The guilty parties are the Council on Foreign Relations people and their neocon collaborators and liberal interventionists who set off to play empire-building after the Cold War and create a New World Order. After the Soviet Union withdrew the Red Army from Europe and split into fifteen nations, and Russia held out its hand to us, we slapped it away and rolled NATO right onto her front porch. Bringing Lithuania, Latvia, and Estonia into NATO did not make America stronger, safer, or more secure. It has surely moved us closer to a military clash with a nuclear power. Enraged Russians turned to a man who would restore respect for their country." Buchanan believes that to the Council on Foreign Relations, America's role in the world is to corral Russia, defend Europe, contain China, isolate Iran, deter North Korea, and battle Al-Qaeda and ISIS wherever they may be, bleeding America's military.

It is this writer's judgment that America is properly encouraged to move away from an interventionist oriented foreign policy, and embark on a non-interventionist foreign policy which will redefine the use of America's military forces. However, we ought not isolate ourselves from the world. Indeed, we cannot. In the 21th century that would have dire consequences.

Americans can expect their federal government to resist this new foreign policy direction, notwithstanding the government's own Global Trend reports that have, for the most part, demonstrated clear and accurate vision into a multipolar world. The US military/government complex has grown so powerful that it is unwilling or unable to think outside of their large box. They have enjoyed the benefits of power for decades. To alter or reduce this structure is a threat to their sense of self. It is natural to resist change and to maintain a strong status quo bias. They will not willingly relinquish their power and the associated benefits.

If the federal bureaucracy is allowed to hold fast to their vast power and size, Americans can be certain of the following consequences:

1. Big government will grow bigger and less responsive to the needs of Americans.
2. The military will become entangled in additional conflicts, resulting in more casualties and continual terrorist attacks on Americans.
3. Our national debt will continue to rise into the tens of trillions, and the American economy will decline much further.

Americans now have an opportunity to take control of their government through their voting power. We are at a critical juncture. The chaos in the presidential primaries is indicative of the pervasive unrest and anger among the electorate.

While we did not learn from our history, it is not yet too late. Some of us still remember listening to President Eisenhower as he delivered his farewell address to the nation, warning us of the increasing power of the military-industrial complex. One can read a draft of his address, including his own penciled-in hand notes, referenced in the endnote. My abridged reduction is as follows:

> Crises there will continue to be . . . There is recurring temptation to feel that some costly action could be the solution to all difficulties . . . a huge increase in newer elements of our defense . . . unrealistic programs to cure every ill . . . Each proposal must be balanced between the clearly necessary and the desirable . . . In government, we must guard against unwarranted influence. The potential for the disastrous rise of misplaced power exists and will persist . . . Research has become more formalized, complex, and costly. A steadily increasing share is conducted for, by, or at the direction of the federal government . . . We must be alert to the danger that public policy could itself become the captive of a scientific-technological elite . . . We want democracy to survive for all generations to come, not become the insolvent phantom of tomorrow.[101]

How prescient were his remarks spoken more than a half century ago! This forewarning by Ike takes on deeper significance because he had served as the Supreme Allied Commander, a warrior elected by the people to the presidency. In the complete text of his address, he said, "Our arms must be mighty, ready for instant action, so that no potential aggressor may be tempted to risk his own destruction," a position that I take in the second half of this chapter. We can anticipate formidable resistance to my proposals. It will come from the military contractors, the large corporations, the powerful lobbyists, the politicians, the bureaucrats, and the agents of all those who will necessarily be displaced, demoted, redeployed, or lessened in stature, power, or income.

It is imperative that under the strong leadership of our newly elected president, the Department of State begin to articulate a refocused foreign policy based on the government's primary mission to protect and defend the American people. A policy that reflects the strong guidance of leaders like Presidents Jefferson, Washington, and Eisenhower and acknowledges that we have already entered into a multipolar world. The United States will have a seat at the table of world leaders. We will join the other powers in responding to challenges. We will influence our partners in how best to deal with humanitarian crises around the globe. We will encourage world leaders to join with us in supporting the International Committee of Red Cross, World Vision International, International Organization for Migration, Refugees International, and similar organizations providing services and resources for those in need.

Resetting our foreign policy in this manner will influence the direction of our military. The US military must be maintained as the strongest military force in the world. However, its mission needs to be refocused. Too many lives are being lost, too many civilians are being killed, too many homes, schools, stores, and workplaces are being destroyed, too much money is being misspent. Our great military has been directed to fight unwinnable battles. We have inflamed too many foreign conflicts and created too many enemies of America where there should be none.

Readers are reminded of President Washington's admonishment to "steer clear of permanent alliances with any portion of the foreign world." We did not heed this advice. There have been sporadic efforts to disengage over the past fifty years, but they have been pushed aside by strong vested interests. In 2007, Ron Paul reintroduced his American Sovereignty Restoration Act, which called for the termination of US membership in the United Nations. Both of Paul's efforts failed in the House.[102] This writer is not ready to recommend the termination of our UN membership, as it would not be timely, given the related proposals that are being set forth in this book. However, the U.N. leadership should begin now thinking through a relocation plan.

The United States gives approximately eight billion dollars to the UN each year in mandatory payments and voluntary contributions. The United States is assessed 22 percent (about $622 million) of the regular budget, and over 28 percent of the peacekeeping budget (about $2.4 billion).[103] The United Nations is a flawed organization and has been largely ineffective in dealing with international conflicts.[104] Numerous reports, audits, and investigations have revealed mismanagement, fraud, and corruption in procurement for UN peacekeeping. UN personnel have been accused of sexual exploitation and abuse in Bosnia, Cambodia, Liberia, and other countries. The United States is the UN's biggest bill payer but is just one of 193 voting members when it comes to demanding honesty, efficiency, and effectiveness in return for its overgenerous payments. The GAO determined that the United States funded 50 percent of the UN's cost regarding alleged man-made global warming.[105] Readers can review a delineation of the pros and cons of US membership.[106] As previously noted, given the diplomatic and military initiatives being urged in these pages, it is not timely to remove the United Nations from American soil.

As one contemplates the serious consequences that have resulted from our alliances and entanglements in foreign lands, it is instructive to read the words of John Kerry in his 1971 testimony before the US Senate Foreign Relations Committee.

> We found that most people did not know the difference between communism and democracy. They only wanted to work in the rice paddies without helicopters strafing them and bombs with napalm burning their villages and tearing their country apart. They wanted everything to do with the war, particularly with this foreign presence of the USA, to leave them alone in peace, and they practice the art of survival by siding with whichever military force was present at a particular time . . . We also found that all too often American men were dying in those rice paddies for want of support from their allies. We saw firsthand how monies from American taxes were used for a corrupt dictatorial regime . . . How do you ask a man to be the last man to die for a mistake? Where are the leaders to end this barbaric war in Vietnam.[107]

This is John Kerry, now secretary of state, who holds his voice as the United States drops bombs on Muslims in villages and rice paddies in Africa and the Middle East in 2016. Might this betrayal of beliefs be related to his quest for the presidency?

The United States' entanglement in Vietnam resulted in the deaths of 58,209 young Americans and several million Vietnamese fatalities. In Korea, 54,246 Americans were killed. These are not just numbers. Know that 112,455 mothers learned that their son had been killed on foreign soil. Some fathers did not know where Korea was located. Mothers wondered why America was at war in Vietnam. Tears rolled down American faces for years.

The United States has not learned enough from this military history. The United States is still paying for those conflicts as we maintain 23,310 American troops in Vietnam and 29,300 troops in South Korea. American soldiers are still being killed in Iraq and Afghanistan. The United States is militarily engaged in Libya, Syria, Yemen, and Somalia, and this causes Muslims and others to hate the United States and inspires terrorists to attack Americans. It must be apparent that these conflicts have been between neighboring states and, within states, often rooted in religious rivalries and long-standing tribal turmoil that is best resolved by the people who understand this history. Equally apparent is the fact that US air strikes, American troops on the ground, and the expenditure of trillions of dollars have not been effective. Many believe that the United States has made conditions worse in these foreign lands.

It is in our national interest for the US military to stand down. We need to disengage from these quagmires of death, destruction, and hatred.

Urging the refocusing of the military mission is within the scope of this book. Restructuring the military is the domain of Pentagon officials, military professionals, and select others with requisite expertise. However, one can set the tone by presenting structural reforms for consideration. Previous proposals should be thought of as a means to set the tone as to the gravity of the American condition.

Policy makers want the military to transform failed states into stable democracies, defeat terrorists, protect sea-lanes, democratize the Middle East, protect Europe and Asia from aggression, respond to natural disasters, and much more.[108] The military needs to focus on protecting Americans and defending America. We need to transition all troops out of Korea, Japan, and Vietnam. Treaties and alliances can be modified or suspended. If it is determined that there are compelling reasons (for example, affording the United States first-strike capability), strategic facilities should remain in place. However, the United States ought never to depend on this location advantage.

Once all diplomatic posts in Africa are closed and replaced by virtual embassies and American citizens have had reasonable time to consider/execute relocation options, the withdrawal of military forces can begin. It is recommended that the Pentagon be ordered to remove all military personnel from the African continent. Consideration should be given using the Base Realignment and Closure (BRAC) model, which was successfully used to close military bases between 1988 and 2005. Military personnel can be redeployed to strengthen bases in the United States (see appendix C).

There will be no easy exit from the Middle East, but disengaging our military is in our national interest. Diplomatic posts converted to virtual embassies should precede the removal of American troops. It is recommended that all military personnel be transitioned from the Middle East and redeployed stateside. Some will argue that the United States created a mess and is obligated to clean it up. The Pentagon does not know how to clean it up, and the timely removal of American troops is the priority.

The North Atlantic Treaty Organization (NATO) was founded in the aftermath of World War II to strengthen international ties among member nations to serve as a counterbalance to the Soviet Union and the Warsaw Pact. It served a purpose then, but the world has changed, and NATO has not kept pace with global developments. Books have been written that document the failures of NATO. The United States' concerns have been both financial and operational.

US Defense secretary Chuck Hagel making his final appearance at NATO as US defense chief delivered a sobering message to the NATO allies when he expressed concern about a possible north-south divide in NATO and urged the alliance to tackle multiple security issues at once rather than focusing on one at a time. Hagel's predecessor, Defense secretary Robert Gates, was more direct in his farewell message to NATO when he stated, "The blunt reality is that there will be a dwindling appetite and patience in the United States Congress, and in the American body politic, to expend increasingly precious funds on behalf of nations that are apparently unwilling to devote the necessary resources to be serious and capable partners in their own defense." He stated further that "the United States is tired of engaging in combat missions for those who don't want to share the risks and the costs."

NATO's mutual-defense guarantee, Article 5, is an agreement that an armed attack against one member is considered an attack against them all. On November 24, 2015, a Russian SU-24 was shot down by Turkish F-16s.[109] Under Article 5, the United States would have been membership-bound to defend Turkey had Russia retaliated with a counterattack. NATO membership could involve US military forces in Brussels (Belgium), Greece, Poland, Croatia, Hungary, et al. America troops ought not to be fighting in regional quagmires. An emboldened Putin can quickly and easily move troops into Estonia. The U.S. will have to decide to support NATO in a military effort to repel Russia or to renege on our mutual defense commitment to NATO. It is only a matter of time when the U.S. will need to determine whether to support NATO by sending American troops into Estonia or Latvia.

The US fiscal 2017 budget includes $3.4 billion for a European Reassurance Initiative. The Pentagon plans to outfit and deploy a brigade-size force that will rotate positions across NATO's frontline, including Poland and the Baltics. The American brigade will be combat-ready and able to call on heavy equipment that the United States will have prepositioned on the continent. NATO has exploited America's noble intentions and generosity and is beginning to drag the United States into military conflicts that are not in our nation's interest. Accordingly, it is recommended that the United States nullify its NATO membership.

Absent US membership, NATO, and the European Union can further militarize the existing Common Security and Defense Policy (CSDP) in preparation for armed conflict in their region. NATO will become revitalized when it is no longer dependent on US military and financial support.

The European Union opened its borders to refugees with reckless disregard for the safety and security of its own people. Now they must fight terrorism in Paris, London, and Brussels. This is not America's problem. The United States is developing its own strategy to manage terrorism at home.

The United States has entered into numerous alliances and multilateral agreements that can be nullified. Legal direction/ counsel can be made available by world-class law firms based in Washington. Experts at the National Defense University and the RAND National Defense Research Institute can be engaged in the development of deactivation plans related to these agreements and alliances. These institutions can also be excellent resources relative to the closing of military bases, as well as diplomatic facilities.

The proposed refocusing of American military forces will not compromise the mission to protect and defend. Military disengagement will render Americans safer, particularly from terrorist attacks. The United States will remain a military superpower. Our military leadership will be in a much better position to focus on activity in North Korea, Iran, China, and Russia.

The United States should initiate cultivating positive relationships with Russia and China and foster mutually beneficial bilateral trade agreements with them. We ought not to allow differences between our democratic government and their communist governments to cause us to not engage them in matters of mutual interest. China is North Korea's main trading partner, accounting for 80 percent of Korea's imports and exports. This trade relationship gives China influence over their Korean ally and could prevent an attack. Russia and China should diplomatically be made to understand that, given our refocused military posture, it may become necessary for the United States to neutralize North Korea or Iran.

Admiral Bill Gortney, commander of US Northern Command and the North American Aerospace Defense Command, stated, "We assess that they [North Korea] have the capability to reach the homeland with a nuclear weapon from a rocket . . . We are ready 24/7, if he [Kim Jong-un] is dumb enough to shoot something at us."[110] He later cautioned that while in antimissile tests, we knocked out seventy-two of eighty-nine missiles, which is impressive. But if one missile got through and targeted Seattle, Phoenix, Denver, or Los Angeles, it would be catastrophic. In the event that North

Korea's behavior triggers the US attack criteria, the United States will seek no approval, as it executes pretargeted surgical strikes on Pyongyang, all combat aircraft, and naval warships, as well as command, control, communication, and financial structures. Russia and the world will understand that the United States acts quickly and decisively to protect and defend the American people.

There is a more severe alternative. The *Wall Street Journal* (May 21–22, 2016) reported the results of a study by Dr. Sagan of Stanford University and Dr. Valentino of Dartmouth College in which they commissioned a survey of a sample of US citizens to explore how they might react to the use of a nuclear bomb on Iran. Participants read a mock news article in which the United States places severe sanctions on Iran over allegations that Tehran has been caught violating the 2015 nuclear deal. In response, Iran attacks a US aircraft carrier in the Persian Gulf, killing 2,403 military personnel (the number of Americans killed by Japan at Pearl Harbor in 1941).

Congress then declares war on Iran, and the president demands that Iran's leadership accept unconditional surrender. US generals give the president two options: mount a land invasion to reach Tehran and force the Iranian government to capitulate (at an estimated cost of twenty thousand American fatalities), or shock Iran into unconditional surrender by dropping a single nuclear weapon on a major city near Tehran, killing an estimated one hundred thousand Iranian civilians (similar to the immediate death toll in Hiroshima).

The results were startling: Under one scenario, 59 percent of US respondents backed using a nuclear bomb on an Iranian city. Even when we increased the number of expected Iranian civilian fatalities twenty-fold to two million, 59 percent of respondents—the same percentage supporting the nuclear attack with the lower death toll—still approved of dropping the bomb. Today, as in 1945, the US public is unlikely to hold back a president who may consider using nuclear weapons in the crucible of war.

This writer believes that if the United States declared war on North Korea and dropped a nuclear bomb on Pyongyang, it would be the war that ends all nuclear wars.

On December 31, 2015, Russia published a revised national security document that named as threats both the United States and the expansion of the NATO Alliance.[111] Further, Russian hackers attacked the e-mails of four thousand US military and civilian personnel. The Pentagon characterized the hack as the most sophisticated cyberbreach in US military history.[112] This requires a diplomatic interaction. And this requires that United States' diplomats know Russian history, understand the culture, and are fluent speakers in the Russian language.[113] Our diplomats (and select military personnel) will be more effective if they engage their Russian counterparts in honest discussion speaking to them in their language. This is a must.

In case there are violations of a higher order, the United States will impose economic sanctions that can be increased with the intent of crippling the weak Russian economy. This should not be necessary, given a new administration, new foreign policy, refocused military, and our withdrawal from NATO. We will have removed the primary impediments to developing a positive relationship with Russia. The United States needs to take the initiative in developing honest collaboration on matters of mutual interest. We can be very helpful to Russia if we view them as an ally and not an enemy. It is not unreasonable to believe that within a decade, we can exchange officers between the Pentagon and the Ministry of Defense. Readers are reminded that an American astronaut and a Russian cosmonaut got along fine with each other for a year (24-7) living in Russia's International Space Station.

Presently, the Pentagon is on course to construct a missile defense shield in South Korea and planning a larger string of military bases around the world to complement our facilities in Europe, Australia, Kenya, Saudi Arabia, and elsewhere. Most of these bases require housing complexes, schools, hospitals, recreational and other accommodations. We do not need military bases in Ethiopia, Cameroon, Burkina Faso, Niger, or Kurdistan. Each planned base will provide for up to five thousand American troops. We cannot afford this expansion[114] which perpetuates U.S. military intervention. Given our recent military experiences, we can anticipate the consequences at home and abroad.

The Pentagon's record demonstrates that it has not been a good steward of our tax dollars. This past year, we read about the 225 million–dollar military blimp that came free of its mooring in Maryland. The helium-filled 242-foot blimp broke power lines, leaving twenty-seven thousand families without power, before it deflated and landed north of Harrisburg, Pennsylvania. The Pentagon built an extraordinarily expensive gas station in Afghanistan. It lost track of five hundred million dollars in weapons and equipment in Yemen. A US Hellfire missile shipped to Europe for a NATO training exercise was unloaded in Cuba. The sensitive Hellfire technology passed through so many hands in different countries in the unscheduled chain of custody that it is unlikely that there will be any accountability.[115] Indeed, there has been none.

Eaglen writes, today almost none of the new military equipment coming online is revolutionary in design or technology; most are merely an upgraded version of something from the Cold War. China's air-to-air missiles outrange those of the US Air Force, and Beijing continues to invest in developing hypersonic missiles, which travel so fast that defending against them would be almost impossible. And in August, the former commander of the army's electronic warfare division said this of the Russians: "We can't shut them down one-tenth to the degree they can us. We are very unprotected from their attacks on our network."[116] It appears that China and Russia are gaining an edge over the United States while we are engaged in military operations in the Middle East to our detriment.

The United States will spend more than six hundred billion dollars on military operations this year. Less than half the money will be spent on defense; the majority of the money will be spent on offensive military operations around the world. The Pentagon needs to begin changing this ratio to reflect the refocused military's defensive priorities. We cannot afford to have our military stuck in the past Cold War mentality. We need to reallocate most of the offensive funds into our cyberwarfare capability. The US Cyber Command is understaffed and underfunded. We should abort the planned deployment of the Terminal High Altitude Area Defense system, which the Pentagon plans to build on South Korea's border with North Korea.[117] South Korea has actually resisted this US-initiated plan, and the Chinese have been pressuring Seoul to drop the plan.[118] Beijing has expressed deep concerns that the missile-defense system, which monitors North Korea, also will also cover parts of China and could thus weaken Beijing's nuclear deterrent. It may be timely to give American citizens an opportunity to vote on whether the U.S. should continue to assume the role of global peacekeeper.

The United States needs to improve its own missile defenses. Our Missile Defense Agency (MDA) is responsible for managing, directing, and executing our Ballistic Missile Defense Program.

Admiral Syring, current director of MDA, stated that we need to improve our discrimination sensors so that we will be able to quickly identify objects in space, and he called for continued support of the Sea-based X-band Radar (SBX) and to move forward with the Long-Range Discrimination Radar program in Alaska.[119] It is apparent that we need to begin making America's defense a priority. We have the money, but we are spending it on offensive worldwide adventures.

We need to fully fund the Ground-Based Midcourse Defense (GMD).[120] We also need to add more interceptors at our GMD bases in California and Alaska. We need to upgrade and deploy our smart submarines. Our intercontinental stealth bombers must be maintained in a perpetual state of readiness. We need to modernize the US nuclear triad weapons being capable of being launched from land, sea, and air. "Modernization now is not an option. It must happen," said Admiral Haney, head of the US Strategic Command. "The Minuteman 3, ICBM has been on constant 24-hour alert since 1970, and has long surpassed its 10-year life expectancy."[121] To the point, the Pentagon is wasting money in counterproductive offensive military activity around the globe and underfunding critically important defensive upgrades here in America.

We should significantly reduce the size of the army and marine corps.

We need to increase soldiers' compensation by rescinding President Obama's executive order, which raised their pay 1.3 percent. All military personnel in pay grades E-1 through E-9 and W-1 through W-5 should be raised 5 percent. At the officer grade levels 0-6 through 0-11, compensation should be raised 9.5 percent. Currently, the military is losing their top leaders to the private sector where compensation often exceeds one million per year. It is recommended that the Pentagon's civilian workforce be reduced by 25 percent.

One congressional review of Pentagon spending estimated that a comprehensive audit of defense spending would likely generate twenty-five billion dollars in annual savings. My calculations suggest that the annual savings would be approximately fifty-five billion dollars. Ted Cruz and Rand Paul are original cosponsors of the Audit Pentagon Act of 2015, a bill that imposes consequences for the Department of Defense if it does not complete a full Pentagon audit.[122]

US military deployments and lethal engagements are a function of powerful entities, each with a vested interest in keeping America engaged in perpetual war. The Pentagon has become a gigantic organism. If it is left unchecked, there is no likelihood that it will self-correct and rein in its own power. The United States has the greatest military in the world, is proud of its achievements and its history, and is led by the country's finest. But they have been misused and sent on wrong missions with one arm tied back. The Pentagon must be repopulated with military professionals who possess a mind-set open to reforming and refocusing the military. They need to understand that they can best protect and defend America by closing most military bases overseas, redeploying personnel, and shifting resources stateside. This is not the military culture of their training and experience, but it is the only way to make America safe. These intelligent officers will soon comprehend the rationale and see the opportunity to distinguish themselves in this new age of the twenty-first century. They will be responsive to the challenge and accept their new mission.

The proposals, initiatives, and plans outlined in this chapter will save lives and will save trillions of taxpayer money over the next decade. US borders will be permanently secured. Illegal immigration will be stopped. Our Mexican and Canadian borders will be impervious to terrorists. And a not-so-unintended consequence will be the severe curtailment of illegal drugs and contraband entering the United States. Addiction rates will be reduced; young lives will be saved. America will become a profoundly better place to live, work, and provide for our children's future. This book is entitled *Transition America* because we need to begin now to transition from our current condition to where we really need to be if America is to be great again. To this end, direction has been provided.

CHAPTER FIVE

Economic Revitalization and Available Health Care

Economic power is the central element of a nation's strength. The US economy is weak. On March 4, 2016, the Bureau of Labor Statistics (BLS) in Washington proclaimed that the unemployment rate had dropped to 4.9 percent. That number should cause people to smile and click their heels. They are not. Rather, they are hunkering down in anticipation of darker times ahead. This collective apprehension is evidenced in sales of home safes, rentals of bank safe-deposit boxes, and the doubling of gun sales. They are fearful that with the national debt approaching twenty trillion dollars, the dollar will decline in value. The average bank interest rate on savings is 0.08 percent.[123] This is not an incentive for bank deposits, and some fear that banks may begin to fail as in 2009. The Federal Deposit Insurance Corporation reported the failures of 140 banks in 2009.

The recent great recession was triggered by the collapse of a trillion-plus-dollar housing bubble, caused by people buying houses in a higher price range than they could afford and mortgages being given to people who were unqualified to carry the steep burden of monthly payments. Just as mortgage lenders were hawking their low-rate, quick-approval mortgages in 2008, car dealerships are now advertising cash-back, no-interest-for-two-years gimmicks in 2016. Are we inflating a car-loan bubble to partner with the trillion-dollar student-loan bubble for a double whack to the economy? Many families are still underwater, with their mortgages being more than their homes are worth.

Notwithstanding the BLS's 4.9 percent unemployment rate, Americans know that there are too few jobs and that the jobs pay too little. Wages have barely increased, and middle-class families are struggling. Everybody who wants to work should be able to find a job within the range of public transportation. Young college graduates ought to be able to find at least entry-level employment instead of returning to the family home. Higher employment rates will cause wages to rise, which will foster consumerism, which will nourish the economy.

Some believe that the economy is the nation's worst enemy, while others believe that the worst enemy is our failing education system. Still others believe it is our unaffordable health care system or the threat of terror attacks. All these enemies have one common cause, big government, which has effectively created each of these threats. We can repair the broken economy, but it will soon begin to falter because the federal government will continue to borrow as it overspends its financial resources. We can reform education, but we will witness the spawning of new innovative programs with catchy acronyms. We can shut down terrorist cells in Philadelphia and New York City but will soon experience terrorist attacks coming out of cities in New Jersey, California, and Michigan.

Readers need to understand that the core illness is in Washington. If we do not treat this underlying illness, we will continue to deal with the symptoms manifested in the economy, health care, education, and terrorism. One must diagnose and treat the underlying cause of a fever. It doesn't matter which of the nation's threats is the worst enemy, because if we do not treat the source in Washington, these threats will continue to fester and rise again to the threat level. It is this dysfunction of government that spawns these threats, and it must be reduced to a manageable size. Federal bureaucrats at the highest levels of government are too removed from the people to have the perspective to make appropriate decisions about their well-being. There are too many federal agencies which are also way too large. These agencies have been politicized and populated with mediocre employees. Understand that there is a point at which there is an inverse relationship between the size of the federal government and the country's economic growth. In other words, given a reduction in the number of federal agencies and in the personnel of departments, institutes, and agencies—there will be an expansion of our economic growth.

Washington has lost the war on poverty, stateside, and lost the war on global poverty as well. The federal government has succeeded in nurturing dependent individuals, dependent families, and dependent foreign states, all to their disadvantage and America's disadvantage. It will require a movement to remediate the federal condition. This grassroots effort needs to be formalized in every county of every state. It must be a movement by the people, for the people, for a healthy downsized federal government.

The national debt exceeds $150,000 per household. We are in a suboptimal economic condition because the government cannot begin to pay the debt down. The reason is that every dollar collected in tax revenue is being used to pay for the massive entitlement costs and the interest on the national debt. It should be noted the China holds approximately $1.3 trillion of the U.S. national debt which is way too much. This has empowered China with significant leverage in global affairs, particularly in international trade. The fact that Americans are becoming accustomed to a 19.4 trillion–dollar national debt and a trillion-dollar 2017 budget and the fact that the national debt increases approximately $2.5 billion every day should set off an alarm. People are accepting this condition as a new economic reality, a new norm. They do so at their own peril. This is not simply a matter of adding additional zeros, lest future generations are faced with a quadrillion-dollar national debt. Remember that it was not bombs that resulted in the demise of the Soviet Union (USSR). It was their broken economy.

Ronald Reagan authorized the Grace Commission (Executive Order No. 12369) to conduct an assessment of waste and inefficiency in the federal government. The commission identified 2,478 specific examples of government waste that could have resulted in savings of $135 billion annually. David Stockman (OMB) had nothing but disdain for the Grace report and did nothing to implement its recommendations.[124] Congress and federal bureaucrats can be expected to undermine or attack any list of recommendations that threatens their power or positions of influence.

When the proposals put forth in this book are fully implemented, the national debt will be reduced to a relatively healthy $8 trillion in a dozen years. For starters, the elimination of all financial and military aid to foreign countries, the closing of diplomatic and military facilities in selected foreign countries, the personnel reductions in the Pentagon and troop levels, the enactment of a required balanced budget every year, and the reductions in social security and health care will take a huge bite out of the debt. Removing all military forces from Africa and the Middle East saves hundreds of billions each year, and it will eliminate terrorist attacks on Americans. When the savings resulting from the proposals specified in chapter 6 are added to the cumulative total, we can expect the national debt will be entirely eliminated by 2035..

A newly elected president with a specific detailed plan for government downsizing reform will require broad-based support in the Senate and the House of Representatives. This will be a challenge because these politicians will have to turn their backs on lobbyists, large donors, and self-interest groups, all of which they have learned to need and to do their bidding. Politicians spend almost half their time raising money, primarily from wealthy individuals and lobbyists who represent industries and organizations that the government is supposed to oversee. The result is that Washington devotes its attention to powerful groups each having a financial, professional, or ideological stake in the workings of big government. The influence of these groups on politics, policy, and decision-making within the halls of government is immense. Legions of government bureaucrats, whose future is geared to the growth of federal power and spending, grow larger and more powerful by spewing out more agency regulations that have had a stifling effect on the growth of our economy.[125]

A September 2015 Gallup poll found that 75 percent of this country thinks that the federal government is corrupt.[126] Campaign finance reform has not worked very well. It makes no sense to require congressmen to run for reelection every two years. They use half their time in office raising money for their next election. We need to lengthen their term in office. While the condition in the Senate is not as dysfunctional, their term in office needs to be adjusted accordingly, with members of the House of Representatives being lengthened to four-year terms and senators being elected to serve seven year terms. This will afford our elected officials adequate time to focus on crafting legislation that is responsive to the needs of government and its people.

Know that state and local governments are in decidedly better condition. They are still largely responsive to the people who elected them to office. However, this is not uniformly true. Readers may recall the decades of corruption in the New York Legislature in Albany. In May, Sheldon Silver, former speaker of the New York Assembly who served under five different governors, was sentenced to a twelve-year prison term. Voters need to be very thoughtful when they contemplate whom they will vote for at every level of government.

Many of the recommendations in this book, when enacted and implemented, will shift a huge responsibility for services to the state and county levels of government. Billions of dollars will be redirected from Washington to each of the fifty states. State governments will need to increase in size, but it will be controlled growth. As one safeguard, it is being recommended that all states that receive federal block grant funds be required to create an Office of State Ombudsman (OSO). Many states already have such an office. However, it is typically small and singularly focused—for example, a children's advocate, property rights advocate, or an aging ombudsman. Depending on the state, these existing offices will become units within the OSO. Further, within the OSO, there will be a required unit to protect whistle-blowers and facilitate the processing of their reports. The OSO will serve as the eyes and ears of the people at the state level.

The federal government needs a new balanced-budget law. It should be a simple legislative amendment to avoid controversy that has inhibited the proper implementation of previous initiatives. If deemed necessary, guidance may be found in the Gramm-Rudman-Hollings Act of 1985 and the Balanced Budget Act of 1997, which was sponsored by John Kasich. It is recommended that Congress enact a new constitutional amendment that requires that federal spending not exceed federal receipts. It must include a provision that prevents Congress from enforcing the amendment by increasing taxes and include a provision covering federal economic emergencies or a declaration of war. The law will require the president to submit a balanced budget each year to Congress.

Most American families find it necessary to have a budget so that they do not overspend their income. We should expect no less of the federal government. Without the proposed amendment, the government will continue on autopilot when it comes to constructing the budget. Decisions, in the main, will be based on the prior year's budget decisions. For the most part, funding will simply be increased. Therefore, most of the federal programs that are deemed necessary and desirable will be moved from Washington to the state and county levels of government or to the private sector All federal departments will be significantly reduced in size by eliminating programs, services, and personnel (for an initial starting point, see appendix D).

When viewing the seemingly endless array of federal agencies, one needs to consider taking either a weedwacker or a flamethrower to the bureaucratic field of the bloated federal agency empire. Readers will be relieved to know that the writer mercifully removed two-thirds of the content from the original draft of this section on the Bureau of Indian Affairs (BIA)! The BIA was selected as an example of the federal mismanagement of agencies because Washington has had 192 years of experience in its effort to improve the functioning of the BIA. It should have taken a few years because the target population being served has historically been comparatively malleable and nonconfrontational with their guardian superiors in Washington.

The Department of Health and Human Services report states, "The FY 2015 Budget requests of $6 billion for the Indian Health Service (IHS) an increase of $228 million or 4 percent over FY 2014."[127] The tribes also receive funds from other departments. The Department of Education spends more than three hundred million dollars a year on Bureau of Indian Education (BIE) schools. The Department of Housing and Urban Development runs the Native American Housing Block Grant Program, which spends approximately eight hundred million dollars. Additional funding comes from the Department of Energy and the Department of Defense. There are also private organizations and foundations that provide financial assistance. And then there is the Indian casino income. Suffice it to state that the plight of Native Americans and the often deplorable living conditions on Indian reservations in 2016 are not due to a lack of money. It has been two hundred years since these Native Americans were forcefully removed from their homes and lands by strange people with rifles. The writer has standing to address the subject.[128]

President Obama submitted his FY 2017 budget proposal to Congress, which increased funding across the board for Indian country: "His request for $13.4 billion for the Dept. of Interior . . . provides critical support for tribal self-determination and economic advancement, including historic transformation of the Bureau of Indian Education (BIE) school system to help improve education for Indian children. Overall next year, the BIA and BIE would see a $137.6 million increase, for a total of $2.9 billion . . . . Included within the IHS funding is $800 million for Contract Support Costs (CSC) and a proposal to reclassify CSC as a mandatory appropriation beginning in FY 2018 . . . . The Tiwahe Initiative would receive $141 million . . . . HUD's funding includes $29 million to the BIA to support tribal communities preparing for and responding to impacts of 'climate change' . . . . The EPA will provide $96.4 million for the Tribal General Assistance Program . . . . Obama acknowledged, the painful history, the broken promises that are part of the past . . . . America has a moral obligation to do right by the tribes."[129]

The manner in which the funding proposal is written—for example, CSC—guarantees that the increase extends well into the next administration, regardless of the outcome of the coming elections. There are other initiatives through the National Institutes of Health, the Offices of Special Education and Rehabilitation Services, the English Language Acquisition and Indian Education, the National Institute of Literacy, the Office of Indian Education Programs (OIEP), and the Family and Child Education (FACE) program, which provides services to American Indian families with children from birth to grade 3 and enables parents to improve their parenting skills.[130]

It appears that excessive funding funneled through too many departments, agencies, and initiatives has created too many problems. This condition has been going on for well over a hundred years. By now, Native American children should be performing very well in schools and colleges. They are not. By now, these children should be enjoying good health. Too many are not.

The gold standard in educational assessment is the National Assessment of Educational Progress. The present study compared results with the two prior longitudinal studies—compared female with male achievement and Native American students with black and white students—and presented results by state and by region. I drilled deeply into the tabular data. Suffice it to note that in 2009, the percentages of Native American students performing at or above the basic level in reading were 50 percent at grade 4 and 62 percent at grade 8. Twenty percent of Native American students at grade 4 and 21 percent at grade 8 performed at or above the proficient level in reading in 2009.

In mathematics, examining the summative data on 8,900 students, the percentages of Native American students performing at or above the basic level were 66 percent at grade 4 and 56 percent at grade 8. Twenty-one percent of Native American students at grade 4 and 18 percent at grade 8 performed at or above the proficient level in mathematics in 2009.

At the advanced level in reading, 4 percent of fourth graders and 2 percent of the eighth-grade students met the standard. In mathematics, 2 percent of the native students in grade 4 and 3 percent of the Native American students in grade 8 were at or above the advanced level.[131]

There was insignificant growth in Native American student-achievement levels during the decade in which the three major studies were conducted. Given the generous expenditure of funds, one would have expected better results. Giving readers a detailed historical overview of the numerous efforts over the past century to provide for the education and welfare of American Indians, Hunt wrote that the history of the BIA for the most part is one of ongoing failures, mismanagement, and even some corruption.[132] The writer shared some anecdotal thoughts in the endnotes.[133]

Decision making among Native Americans is conditioned by culture, race, and unique life experiences. An understanding of these variables is a prerequisite to understanding their decisions whether to read and study, experiment with drugs, or aspire to a career in law or business. When I think about the variables that may explain the disappointing student-achievement results, attention is focused on intelligence, culture, and government.

Despite the work of Charles Murray linking racial differences with intelligence, I see no convincing evidence of that relationship.[134] Cultural differences can account for a significant portion of the disappointing student performance. In the next chapter, I present differential achievement data across several cultures. But I believe the overriding variable is government. It is too removed from the target population. There are too many programs and agencies involved, and there is too much money in play.

One example, the Office of Indian Energy Policy and Programs is charged with directing and implementing energy planning and programs that assist tribes with energy development and electrification of Indian lands and homes. It should be relatively straightforward to install solar panels and extend power lines into the reservations in 2016. Yet on the Pine Ridge Reservation in South Dakota, almost 40 percent of the people live without electricity. Susan Rice highlighted President Obama's tribal energy initiatives in her remarks before the UN Permanent Forum on Indigenous Issues in 2011. And Kimberly Teehee, White House senior policy advisor for Native American Affairs, described a Tribal Summit that brought together more than 350 participants, including tribal leaders and high-ranking cabinet officials, to interact directly.[135] It would be challenging to get 350 people to interact directly with high-ranking cabinet officials. Too many important people flying across the country to discuss too many Indian initiatives, costing too much money, which should have been spent putting up power lines on the Indian reservations, one might think.

If you want to know why American Indians have the highest rates of poverty of any racial group and why suicide is the leading cause of death among Indian men (on the Pine Ridge Reservation, there were seventeen suicides in one month in 2014),

Naomi Schaefer Riley's book entitled *The New Trail of Tears: How Washington Is Destroying American Indians* will be out in hardcover on July 26, 2016. The school dropout rate on the reservation is over 70 percent.

In 2013, the principal of the Wounded Knee School fired all ten of her teachers and rehired only two. The eight who were let go were from Teach for America—some with Ivy League degrees, all with a commitment to help the children at Pine Ridge. When the former president of the Oglala Sioux was asked about the teachers fired, she replied, "I don't think any of them were native." Clearly, there are tribal leadership issues on many of the reservations.

Native American children are underachieving in their public schools. American Indians have the highest prevalence of substance abuse and dependence among the racial and ethnic groups in the United States.[136][137][138] These children have slight chance of achieving the American dream; for too many of them, it is only a dream. Alcohol addiction has plagued Indian reservations for decades with crippling consequences, one lost generation after another. There have been thousands of substance-use programs made available by government agencies for American Indians and Alaska Native children. There is a disconnect, and it does not have to be this way. In New Jersey, in 1992, there was a three-year research study that linked specific interventions into the infrastructure of a school district as a substance-use prevention model. There was no funding, no research staff. The goal was to prevent teenagers from even trying drugs. It made sense to try to prevent drug use rather than treat drug addiction later. The success of the program was recognized at an award ceremony in Washington.[139] Results are achievable. The federal government has created too many addiction-treatment programs with very little accountability. The results are absolutely disgraceful.

The federal government established the Office of Indian Trade in 1806; that was 210 years ago. The BIA was created as a federal agency in 1824! The government has had two hundred years to figure out how best to help the Native Americans. The agency has expanded over the years and now employs nine thousand federal personnel to work on the Indian problem. They just cannot figure out how to do things right. For example, they constructed a fish hatchery, but after fourteen years of funding, no fish were ever hatched. The BIA spent nine million dollars on a public ferryboat, but the funds went to a private tour boat business. BIA received $2.4 million to build a road, but the Inspector General was unable to locate any of the work that was supposed to have been completed for the Indians.

You know things must be very bad if the *New York Times* devotes an editorial to the BIA condition, writing, "It now appears that a ring has long existed in the Indian Bureau in Washington for the express purpose of covering up these frauds, and facilitating others." The *NYT* expressed this outrage on December 12, 1868![140] At the outset of this BIA agency section, it was noted that more than half the content was removed. It included ten pages of Indian programs and initiatives that should be abolished. For example, rescind Executive Order No. 13592—strengthening Tribal Colleges and Universities, signed by President Obama on December 2, 2011. Suffice it to state that this "national disgrace" (coined by the Inspector General in 2004), this scandal-ridden empire, should be entirely dismantled, and a single functional agency created to actually enable Native Americans to achieve self-determination and rid the reservations of drug/alcohol addiction and provide quality education from preschool through college. We can achieve these results without nine thousand employees and without spending hundreds of billions of taxpayers' dollars. It will take a few years, but not 192 years.

This one agency, BIA, was used as an example of the redundancy, mission creep, mismanagement, waste and misconduct, and very poor results to be found among the other 429 federal agencies. The reader will be spared an additional fourteen pages of the writer's rationale for eliminating specific agencies and merging others.[141] With one exception, thoughts relative to the EPA will be shared. The next president should probably take the flamethrower approach. And it is also important to look beyond the regular agencies and reassess the purpose and funding of the US Institute of Peace,[142] the Legal Services Corp,[143] the Global Solutions component of the Graduate School USA, and the National Endowment for Democracy.[144] [145]

The Department of Veterans Affairs is a national disgrace. It continues to underserve our veterans under both Republican and Democratic administrations. Too many veterans have made it home from war, and have died waiting for their VA appointment. This writer is not alone in frustration for not being able to tackle the Dept. of Veterans Affairs. My congressman, Dr. Roe, is an active member of the House Committee on Veterans Affairs where he sits on the Oversight and Investigations and Health Subcommittee. Phil Roe is a veteran who served two years in the United States Medical Corps. He is quoted as recently stating, "Even GOP presidential nominee Donald Trump would face challenges changing the Veterans Administration if he became president." Roe points out that the VA is a gigantic organization with a $180 billion budget. Money is not the problem; size is the problem. Mismanagement has resulted in widespread mediocrity, and not inconsiderable incompetency among the 365,000 employees. Since 1992, we have had twelve secretaries of veterans affairs.

Congressman Roe will likely chair the VA House Committee next year. I take pause when he states that nothing is going to change immediately because it is such a large organization, and to change something that big is going to take 10 to 20 years. This is an affront to our nation's wounded warriors. It should be noted that in a recent conversation with Congressman Roe, he did delineate many of the reasons for the difficult extended timeline. I was surprised to hear that he even has to deal with resistance to change from recognized veterans organizations. In chapter seven, I propose that a non-governmental firm such as Booz Allen Hamilton he contracted to analyze the VA's condition and make recommendations to finally remedy the widespread problems.

The Environmental Protection Agency (EPA) has an important mission to accomplish. It is a truism that the larger an entity becomes, the more complex it becomes and more prone to failures. The EPA ignored their own written warnings and then proceeded to contaminate the Animas River in Colorado. The Gold King Mine blunder was a 2015 environmental disaster that spread contamination into Colorado, New Mexico, Utah, and the Navajo Nation. The heavy metals and acid-mine drainage changed the river's color to bright orange. The EPA had warned themselves twice. An EPA work order read: "Conditions may exist that could result in a blowout of the blockages and cause a release of large volume of contaminated mine waters and sediment from inside the mine."[146] And that is precisely what happened when the EPA executed a work order at the Gold King Mine. About two hundred thousand people in three states drink water from the four-hundred-mile Animas and San Juan River system, which feeds into the Colorado River, which supplies much of the Southwest. Residents worry whether a buildup of metals will pose health threats. The EPA estimates that 880,000 pounds of heavy metals spilled into the Animas River.

Again, the EPA ignored early warnings in Flint, Michigan. Parents began complaining in April 2014 about their drinking water's color, taste, and odor. Childhood lead exposure causes a reduction in intellectual functioning and IQ, an increased risk of aggression and hyperactivity. Children with elevated levels of lead in the blood are more likely as adults to commit crimes, be imprisoned, be unemployed, and be dependent on government services.[147] Many families have already filed lawsuits against numerous government entities. When these lawsuits are resolved, taxpayers will have a very large bill to pay. Congressional hearings have shown that a series of government errors at the local, state, and federal level caused Flint's lead-contaminated water, but the EPA is trying to pretend it had nothing to do with it.[148]

USA Today journalists used the EPA's Safe Drinking Water Information System to conduct their own investigative study.[149] Since 2012, nearly two thousand water systems across the United States have found elevated lead levels in tap water samples.[150] The EPA estimates that about 7.5 million lead service lines remain in use nationwide. As these lines continue to age, they are more likely to corrode and deposit lead in the drinking water.[151] Lead in tap water has been found in California, Texas, Pennsylvania, New York, and New Jersey. In Newark, New Jersey, seventeen thousand children are being tested for lead poisoning after elevated levels of the toxin were found in the drinking water. These old pipe conditions exist in almost every large city in America. These conditions exist in American communities, while we are spending millions of dollars purifying water in Africa.

The EPA has been preoccupied with climate change. It has decimated the natural coal industry in Virginia, Pennsylvania,

Kentucky, and West Virginia. EPA regulations have dealt a blow to electric power plants across the country, cutting into earnings and causing an increase in consumers' utility bills. Fifty coal companies have been forced into bankruptcy. The EPA's regulations on clean power and clean air have resulted in stay orders by the US Court of Appeals. There is evidence of climate change, though there is considerable disagreement among recognized scientists. This is a global issue and should be addressed by a consortium led by China and India. The United States would be expected to be a member, and this would be entirely consistent with our nation's newly defined role in a multipolar world. The EPA should shift its focus away from spending billions of dollars and using thousands of federal employees to fight global warming and concentrate on the lead-contaminated drinking water that is currently poisoning American children.

Social Security is on an unsustainable path. Levin notes that it is hemorrhaging money. The national birthrate does not provide enough working people from whom money can be transferred to subsidize beneficiaries, and most individuals do not have enough money to get them through severe economic times.[152] Currently, there are sixty-five million Americans receiving social security benefits. They will receive approximately $900 billion in social security benefits in 2017, according to the FY 2017 Budget Overview. The aged population is increasing faster than the other age groups, and older people are living longer and becoming more dependent. The amount of money coming from employees into social security has not kept pace with the increasing number of retirees who are receiving benefits. This has created an unsustainable condition.

Social security benefits are relatively modest with the average monthly retirement benefit in June 2015 being $1,335 per month.

For many elderly retirees, that is not adequate. The United States ranks thirty-first among thirty-four developed countries in the percentage of a median worker's earnings that the public-pension system replaces.[153] Being responsive to the needs of the elderly and our relative position on benefits compared with the other developed nations, it is recommended that regular monthly benefits be increased by 3 percent for all recipients. Those who have earned higher incomes and paid more into the system ought not to be denied the increase.

Now that Social Security is in a deeper hole, attention is directed to the fix. Medicare will be covered under the section on "Available Health Care." First, it is proposed that the cap on taxable social security earnings be raised from the current $118,500 as follows: $120,000 in 2018, $122,000 in 2020, $125,000 in 2023, and $129,000 in 2027.

Presently, the earliest age at which a person can start receiving social security retirement benefits is age sixty-two. The following proposed age increases should be phased in by monthly increments over a period of ten years: age sixty-three by 2018, age sixty-four by 2024, and age sixty-five by 2028. The age at which a person is eligible to retire with full social security benefits also needs to be adjusted. For individuals born between January 1, 2000 and December 31, 2005, the age should be reset to sixty-eight; born between January 1, 2006 and December 31, 2016, reset to sixty-nine; and for people born January 1, 2017 and thereafter, the reset age will be seventy. Congress should also enact legislation that provides financial incentives for individuals who choose to continue to work beyond the age at which they will be eligible to receive full benefits.

The requirements and procedures for determining an individual's eligibility to receive disability benefits require attention, though this writer has no remedy. The Congressional Budget Office (CBO) projects that under current law, the Disability Insurance Trust Fund will be exhausted in fiscal year 2017, and the Old-Age and Survivors Insurance Trust Fund will be exhausted in 2032.[154] The Social Security Administration administers the Supplemental Security Income (SSI) program and the Social Security Disability Insurance (SSDI) program. Both programs provide assistance to people with disabilities. The SSI program pays benefits based on financial need.[155] It is designed to help aged, blind, and disabled people who have little or no income. It provides money to meet basic needs for food, clothing, and shelter. The program is funded by general tax revenues. It is a necessary program, with very few people receiving undeserved benefits. SSI should remain in place. The SSDI program has a few vulnerabilities. It is not illegal for veterans with a disability rating of at least 50 percent to collect retirement benefits from the Department of Defense and disability compensation from the Department of Veterans Affairs and SSDI all at the same time. An example cited is a fifty-four-year-old who retired in 1997 after twenty years in the military and collected $122,887 in total benefits in 2013.[156]

Whether it is the SSA or the VA disability program, word does get around as to how best to game the system. The medical disability requirements procedure to determine eligibility for benefits has been a weak spot in the SSA program. Before the Black Lung Benefits program was transferred from SSA to the Department of Labor in 2002, there had been long-standing abuse of the system. Individuals who had never been near a coal mine received black lung benefits for years. The law was written for miners who were totally disabled from pneumoconiosis arising from employment in or around the nation's coal mines.[157] There was barroom conversation about how the program worked and how to qualify for the monthly checks.[158] This egregious behavior may be less widespread, but it is still happening and should be addressed by those with program responsibility.

Ronald Reagan stated, "Extreme taxation, excessive controls, oppressive government competition with business, frustrated minorities, and forgotten Americans are not the products of free enterprise. They are the residue of centralized bureaucracy, of government by a self anointed elite." He also said, "Taxation is the art of plucking feathers without killing the bird. It's time they [congress] realize that the bird just doesn't have any feathers left."[159] Taxation must be addressed now.

Senator Cruz's tax proposal states that the IRS is such a twisted, bloated organization that it must be abolished. It cannot simply be downsized. There is no doubt that the IRS has grown way too large and has been plagued by scandals, mismanagement, and a lack of accountability. The federal tax code is 74,608 pages! It can, and should, be reduced to a hundred pages. Einstein said, "The hardest thing in the world to understand is the income tax." And that was more than a half century ago.

The federal government does not have a tax problem; it has a spending problem. We will significantly reduce the spending by implementing the *Transition America* recommendations. Now it is time to reduce the taxes. The IRS should be reduced in size, function, and funding. Under the proposed tax model, the IRS's 82,203 employees can be reduced to one thousand and moved as a unit to the Department of Treasury. We should establish a revenue retrieval/ tax fraud unit within the Department of Justice.

It is proposed that a simple flat tax model set the income tax rate at 10 percent for everyone required to pay taxes. An estimated 45 percent of American households—roughly seventy-seven million—presently pay no federal individual income tax, according to data for the 2015 tax year from the Tax Policy Center.[160] It is important that every wage earner have a stake in America. This will spur economic growth by eliminating loopholes and broadening the tax base. After seven years of sluggish growth, the economy staggering along at 2 percent needs to be stimulated.

The Tax Foundation estimated that the Cruz 10 percent flat tax plan would result in 4.8 million more full-time equivalent jobs.[161] I make no such claim but will welcome a similar outcome. It has been estimated that about three hundred billion dollars a year in taxes go uncollected with the IRS in its current iteration. By downsizing the IRS and reforming the tax code, this condition will be remediated. Under the proposed tax model, there will be no tax on earned interest. The rate on capital gains and dividends will be reduced to 10 percent.

The model calls for a consumption tax in the form of a 3 to 5 percent national sales tax. It should be recognized that within chapters 2 through 6, there are recommendations affecting multiple revenue streams and offering significant reductions in expenditures. I did not enjoy the luxury of time to run all the numbers, and would welcome readers with expertise to address this important task. It is likely that an adjustment in the 3 to 5 percent national sales tax range may be necessary. It is, however, a fair method for distributing the tax burden. Further, it is urged that consumption tax experts recommend an appropriate increase in federal tax on drinking alcohol and the winnings from casino gambling and lotteries.

Large corporations are moving to foreign countries at an increasing exit rate. Pfizer is merging with Allergan in a $160 billion deal to reduce its tax bill by moving to Ireland, which has a more corporate friendly tax rate. Johnson Controls estimates that its move to Ireland will result in $150 million savings each year.

Carrier Corporation is moving manufacturing to Mexico. General Electric is selling its entire appliance division to Electrolux of Sweden for $3.3 billion. Burger King said it will buy Tim Hortons of Canada and move its tax headquarters to Canada. Corporate tax inversions will continue to increase. Apple and numerous other corporations have found other ways to minimize taxes in the United States by keeping profits overseas. It is estimated that the foreign cash hoard of American companies has reached $1.95 trillion.[162]

Congress appears to be oblivious to this grand corporate exodus of production facilities, jobs, and tax dollars to foreign countries. The United States needs to stop this hemorrhaging. We need to incentivize corporations to bring the two trillion dollars being stashed overseas back to the United States. We need to eliminate the regulatory requirements that agencies have imposed on American corporations. Many of our multinational corporations have production facilities in multiple tax jurisdictions and shift their profits to their tax advantage. These corporate moves result in American jobs being performed by workers in foreign countries.[163] The International Tax Competitiveness Index has the United States ranked a low thirty-two out of thirty-four industrialized nations. The Organization for Economic Cooperation and Development has the United States coming in dead last of thirty-four countries on the variable of taxing corporate income.[164] The US corporate tax rate average is about 35 percent, and on top of that, they pay an additional but much lower tax on their production in the foreign countries. It is proposed that the federal corporate tax rate be changed to an average rate of 16 percent, with a range from 12 percent to 19 percent, depending on the amount of taxable income. Further, an independent body should be commissioned to evaluate all the strategies/loopholes that corporations have been using to reduce their taxes and make specific recommendations to eliminate them.

Small businesses having fewer than five hundred employees are being constrained by far too many government regulations and licensing requirements at both the state and federal levels. They need relief from all the reporting forms and paperwork. Further, the small entrepreneurs need relief and encouragement. Family-developed businesses with a half-dozen employees are too often harassed with regulations. Many are driven out of business; some move their business into the underground economy, thereby denying tax revenue to the state and federal governments. These small entrepreneurs and the larger small businesses combined generate 65 percent of new jobs. Over 50 percent of the working population works in small business.[165] Government needs to become business-friendly at all levels. When implemented, the foregoing recommendations will effectively reenergize the struggling economy. Manufacturing will be rekindled. Jobs will be created, and wages will rise. There will be a corresponding reduction in unemployment and welfare benefits.

Trade agreements need to be reassessed, with attention focused on NAFTA, FTAA, and TTP, as they are not in our national interest. We need to engage a world-class international law firm to guide the United States in exiting the thicket of multilateral trade agreements to which we are tied. The United States can stand fast and accept retaliation. Though the law is murky, a president can probably pull the United States out of the WTO or NAFTA on six months' notice, says Gary Horlick, a globally recognized veteran trade lawyer.[166]

America's interests will be better served by negotiating bilateral trade agreements with Mexico and Canada. These agreements can be completed expeditiously and used as a template for additional bilateral negotiations. The United States should develop/maintain bilateral agreements with Brazil, China, India, Israel, Russia, Cuba, Chile, Peru, Jamaica, Korea, Vietnam, Columbia, and Australia. We may need to negotiate additional bilateral trade agreements with African states to gain access to mineral resources. Trade agreement priority should be given to those nations that were impacted most by the elimination of US financial aid. We should not enter into a trade-dependency relationship with any foreign country. They ought not to depend on us, nor we on them. Obviously, they can depend or count on the United States honoring every detail of a bilateral agreement. The United States has the economic resources to satiate all its import needs. In case Canadian lumber does not meet all our needs, the United States may need to pay to import Jamaican cedar or Brazilian mahogany.

The United States can manufacture clothing, cars, computer chips, kitchen appliances, televisions, and smartphones. American workers are trainable and capable of manufacturing 90 percent of the products that are currently being imported. In fact, our largest imports should be raw materials but fewer cut roses from Peru. We need to get government to stimulate manufacturing by subsidizing the construction of manufacturing plants. I recommend dedicated block grants to individual states to effectively accomplish this economic necessity. Wages will increase. Americans will have the earnings power and income tax relief to pay higher prices for American products. Employment will increase.

The economy will benefit if we return to a standard forty-hour work week. Too many workers are settling for part-time employment. Too many Americans find it necessary to hold two separate jobs which is an inefficient use of the labor force. Workers must orientate themselves to two different work environments, procedures, and supervision structures. Millions of Americans have given up on seeking employment. Given the odeious constraints upon employers imposed by Obamacare and medicare, too many jobs are capped at thirty hours per week. Under the proposed available health care plan and the repositioning of medicare, employees will be able to return to a traditional forty hour work week.

Congress is also working on legislation to lift the 30-hour threshold. Other initiatives set forth in these pages will enable America to return to a manufacturing-based economy which will create desirable employment opportunities across the country. The economy will be returned to a robust condition, as we revive the "made-in-America" creedo.

Readers should have noted that Cuba was included as a prospective bilateral trade partner. The US Congress should lift the Cuban trade embargo. Cuba is not an enemy of America. The Iranian leadership and North Korea are our enemies. Cuba has a different form of government, and that may not be long-lived. Russia and China also have different forms of government, and they are not our enemies. The Cold War ended in 1991. The missiles were removed from Cuba in 1962. Given that the median age in Cuba is 41.22 years, most Cubans were not yet born in 1962. Most Americans do not remember the two weeks in October 1962.

Puerto Rico should absolutely not be bailed out. Statehood should be encouraged by federal decision-making for that magnificent island and its American citizens; dependency discouraged. Unfortunately, we can expect Congress to buckle under and craft a bailout plan, and the holders of this massive Puerto Rican debt and taxpayers will suffer the financial loss. The United States will have perpetuated yet another unhealthy dependency relationship.

Creating jobs while waiting for American manufacturing to kick in will require an assist from the government. We need a program similar to the Works Progress Administration (WPA) approved by Congress in 1935 to help lift the country out of the Depression. It is recommended that Congress enact Work America Relief (WAR) legislation to create jobs for American workers—WAR can be funded with repatriated monies made available from the government downsizing initiatives detailed in previous chapters. Money that had been budgeted for financial aid to foreign countries will be used in America to create jobs. The funds gained from military base closings, the elimination of federal regulatory agencies, and the downsizing of the federal bureaucracy will be redirected to WAR. The program can begin with the replacement of lead water pipes found in most older American cities. This will create approximately twenty thousand jobs for plumbers, carpenters, and laborers.

A major portion of WAR funds will be allocated to every state in the form of block grants to repair and replace America's infrastructure. Many of our bridges have degraded by age and cannot pass a structural stress test. Our nation's docks and piers are too often resting on rotting wood, degraded concrete, and rusting metal. Many of the nation's airports have not been maintained or upgraded. Parking facilities and intra-terminal transit need to be brought into the twenty-first century.

The list of needs and jobs is endless. States and counties are closer to the local infrastructure and the vast pool of unemployed workers. They can best align job placement and training with infrastructure and employment needs. There will be a need for laborers, masons, carpenters, electricians, landscapers, welders, et al. Existing and new regional job-training centers must gear up to equip workers with these trade skills and technical competencies.

Millions of good-paying jobs will be available for workers. They will need reliable transportation to get to work sites and job-training centers. We need to expand inexpensive public transportation so that workers need not rely on Uber drivers.

It is recommended that Congress enact legislation to raise the federal minimum hourly pay rate. The rate should be raised to nine dollars per hour in 2018 and increased one dollar each successive year, achieving the federal minimum hourly pay of fifteen dollars by 2024.

The Veterans Affairs officers must be directed to transition the returning veterans into the workforce or job-training programs. We need to promote science research in biotechnology, gene therapy, stem cell research, and nanotechnology. The corporate culture needs to be disrupted. They have a huge stake in the future of the American economy. They can play a key role in revitalizing the economy, which will add dollars to their bottom line. We need corporate leaders like Jack Welch, Mark Cuban, and the deceased Andy Grove. Individuals with their type of mind-set, integrity, and national allegiance can lead the way.

The United States has spent hundreds of billions of taxpayer dollars fighting HIV/AIDS, poverty, and drug addiction in foreign countries. Millions of Americans suffer and die from these same afflictions. Later in this chapter, there are recommendations to create community health centers that will create jobs for health-care personnel. The repatriated monies will be used to hire physicians, nurses, medical technologists, and pharmaceutical personnel to diagnose and provide medical treatment for Americans with health issues. The effective treatment plans and protocols developed to treat these issues will be made available to foreign countries as models so that they can replicate them for treating their own populations.

The war on poverty has been a well-intentioned failure over the last half century. The US welfare system consists of over eighty programs that provide cash, food, housing, medical care, and social services to poor and lower-income Americans. Total annual spending on these programs reached one trillion dollars in 2015.[167] Notwithstanding the fact that trillions of dollars have been spent on these poverty programs or the fact that they have been evaluated hundreds of times over the past fifty years, they have failed to accomplish their mission. They have created a culture of dependency. The goal of welfare should not be to reduce poverty through an even larger welfare state. The goals should be to increase self-sufficiency (having an income above poverty level without relying on government welfare aid), enhance productive participation in society, and improve personal well-being and upward mobility.[168] It is largely the easy money given to welfare recipients and Native Americans that unfortunately enables them to live comfortably without having to work. The manner in which these programs function is debilitating to the recipients. There is very little incentive to provide for oneself and family.

The government's largesse actually serves as a disincentive to seek employment, engage in job training, or become serious about acquiring an education. Too many healthy children are born into the welfare system, which creates a welfare mentality. For these children and their children and grandchildren, it has become a way of life. The current welfare program weakens the institution of marriage, and destroys the cohesive family. The government's misguided programs of generosity have spawned a culture of poverty and dependency—quite the opposite of what they should be fostering. One needs to look no further than the century of government programs intended to foster and develop the self-determination of Native Americans. They too have learned to be dependent.[169]

The government lost the war on poverty, regardless of the glowing periodic evaluations. One ought not to deny reality. Why should it be so difficult to teach people the value of work, education, and independence? The principal mechanisms of prosperous self-sufficiency are work, earnings, and marriage. A healthy marriage is one of the most important factors contributing to personal happiness and in promoting the upward mobility of children. Since the beginning of the war on poverty, marriage has nearly been wiped out in many low-income communities. Replacing husbands with welfare checks has degraded personal well-being for men, women, and children in low-income neighborhoods. By promoting healthy marriage, they will enhance positive participation in society, increase upward mobility, and improve personal well-being, thereby reducing the likelihood of future dependence and welfare expansion.[170]

In the late 1960s, the Moynihan report called America's attention to the plight of the black family, in particular, the single-mother families. In 1969, I asked a black professor what he thought of the report, and his reply was "Moynihan is intellectually dishonest." Moynihan acknowledged in the report that three centuries of injustice had brought about deep-seated structural distortions in the life of the Negro American.

In 1968, about 6 percent of white children and 29 percent of black children lived in single-mother homes. In 1965, 26 percent of black children and 4 percent of white children were born outside of marriage. In 2014, 50 percent of black children and 19 percent of white children were born outside of marriage.[171] Black nuclear families at one time were the norm; now they are the exception. Our antipoverty and welfare programs have spawned a culture of poverty and dependence and have perpetuated the broken-family syndrome.

It is my studied judgment that the government's antipoverty/welfare program cannot be fixed. It is too entrenched in the culture of poverty and has become a part of the problem, not the solution. Social workers and caseworkers have overidentified with the target population. Program directors and managers will continue to protect their comfortable positions. They have a vested interest in maintaining their programs, with occasional tweaks around the edges. Program evaluators often develop relationships with program officials, as both enjoy benefits associated with positive summative reports.

The antipoverty/welfare condition is symptomatic of what ails Washington. It has grown too large over many years. The only remedy is to drastically reduce the size of the federal government. Accordingly, all antipoverty and welfare programs are to be phased out over a period of five to seven years, with all responsibility moved to the state level. The services will be administered by each county. At this level, the personnel will primarily be individuals in or near their place of employment. They will soon know the benefit recipients and the actual severity of their plight. Benefits will be apportioned accordingly. Most importantly, the undergirding mission will be to restore recipients to a productive position in the workplace and in society whereby they can begin to move up the ladder of social mobility and thereby gain a positive, wholesome sense of self as they achieve financial independence. It can be done, must be done. There is no viable alternative.

This brings the writer to the thorny issue of health care. The Affordable Care Act (ACA) has already fallen victim of big government. The United States spends twice as much money on health care than most other countries. The insurance and pharmaceutical industries had too much involvement in shaping ACA to blend with their financial interests. Most Americans are finding that they cannot afford the monthly insurance premiums and high annual deductibles. ACA has become an unwieldy large requirement that is too costly and too removed from the people. It is a complicated mess of paperwork for families as well as the medical professionals. Congress needs to abolish the Affordable Care Act. Individual Americans should have the right to decide for themselves whether or not they need to purchase health insurance. The federal government has become too intrusive in the lives of its citizens.

America needs to transition out of ACA and return to the system in place prior to ACA that, for the most part, consisted of individual employer-based options. Going forward, most Americans will continue to receive medical coverage under an employer option but will have the right to access services in the proposed Available Health-Welfare Centers (AHWC) model. The model will be challenging to operationalize. It is doable. With a determined mission, Americans walked on the moon in 1969! AHWC returns health care decision making directly to the people. The centers will make multiple services available to all Americans. It is expected that families having a net worth in excess of one million dollars will likely only access emergency or special services. Medicaid will be administered by the welfare component of AHWC. Medicare billing will be worked out by professionals, though no unresolvable transition issues are foreseen.

Currently, the Community Health Center (CHC) is the dominant model for federal grant funding for primary care in the country's health care safety net. CHCs are designated as Federally Qualified Health Centers (FQHC) and receive federal funding under section 330 of the Public Health Service Act, which grants them special payment rates under Medicare and Medicaid. There are now more than 1,250 FQHCs, with more than eight thousand delivery sites in all fifty states.[172] The AHWC model builds on this existing structure. And there are literally thousands of other public and semipublic health centers, including the 4,200 family planning centers.[173] As of February 2015, there were 4,084 Medicare-certified rural health clinics.[174] There are nearly five thousand hospitals in the AHA directory.[175] And there are numerous private medical facilities not included in these data. The point is that the country has an abundance of medical facilities in place. A comprehensive medical-health services structure presently exists.

The proposed Available Health and Welfare Centers (AHWC) model will provide complementary and expanded services to the same consumers. This is a comprehensive services program that places medical, welfare, and employment services at the local level, giving individuals direct access in a timely manner. It takes the best practices developed under the Personal Responsibility and Work Opportunity Reconciliation Act and the Job Training Partnership Act. It works closely with the local community colleges, private organizations, and for-profit service providers. It is a comprehensive facility that will provide the full gamut of medical, welfare, and employment services. It will be staffed by local professionals who understand the needs and peculiarities of the people they serve. The physical facilities' size, design, and configuration will be based on existing local facilities and the size and needs of the population being served. Regional centers will be established at the county level and smaller community centers at the local level.

Over a period of seven years, ACA will be entirely phased out and AHWC phased in. In the not-too-distant past, it would have been difficult to imagine the network of Amazon packaging and distribution centers across the country. Physical facilities can be designed to meet clearly defined needs. When there is a dedicated mission, the government can land people on the moon and certainly provide structures and staff to deliver specific human services.

Essential staffing requirements will be the same across centers. There will be operational differences. Regional centers in urban locations will be open 24-7, while suburban and rural centers will be configured and staffed in accordance with community requirements. Professional personnel will include physicians (diagnostic/emergency), nurse specialists with experience in pediatrics and geriatrics, social caseworkers, clinical psychologists, x-ray and lab technicians, welfare agents, employment specialists, intake officers, and case managers. American taxpayers provide more than adequate funding for these services.[176] The president's FY 2017 budget request for Employment and Training Administration (ETA) was $10.3 billion.[177] The FY 2017 nutrition assistance program (SNAP) was $81.7 billion.[178] AHWC will save billions in government spending.

The proposal requires organization, communication, and coordination. Intake officers and case managers will have mission-critical responsibilities. Intake officers will create individual computer-system case files and assign a case manager for each person. Case managers will coordinate and integrate services being provided for each client. They will perform individual need assessments, follow-up, and ongoing case management, tracking the individual's progress throughout the person's involvement with center services and personnel. Caseloads must be functionally reasonable. Staff will attend regularly scheduled meetings to keep services aligned. The serviced population will include consumers from all social/economic strata, though the majority will be from the low- and mid-income strata. The system will be designed to be as simple as is functionally reasonable. The welfare and employment personnel will continually promote the value of marriage and family, work, and education.

There will be an emphasis on diagnosis, early detection, and prevention. Too many men are still dying from prostate cancer; too many women are dying from breast cancer. Family planning will be available at every center. Upon request, age-appropriate females will be provided with family planning information, including optional sterilization with appropriate referrals. All mental health personnel will be alert for suicidal ideation and terrorist symptomatology. All personnel will be alert for addiction/ dependency symptoms. The FY 2017 budget request for national drug-control programs was $15.8 billion.[179] Drug addiction is destroying lives and families. Sentencing guidelines need to be changed so that drug dealers receive punishingly long sentences and addicts are provided with recovery treatment.

The Available Health and Welfare Centers (AHWC) proposal will understandably be criticized as naive, undoable, and radical by the insurance and pharmaceutical industries, as well as by the Washington bureaucracy, which has a vested interest in maintaining the status quo. Under AHWC, physicians and related health and clinical personnel will fare much better economically than they did under ACA.

AHWC is a creatively bold and transformative model. It is an important component of this writer's effort to downsize the federal government and put a stop to the uncontrollable spending of taxpayer monies in Washington. It is important to also understand that all the initiatives in this book are interrelated, including national security, foreign policy, military strategy, health, education, and welfare.

The implementation of AHWC will require unique leadership in Washington. It requires a leader who has not been indoctrinated into the Washington culture and establishment. It requires a leader with a demonstrated record of experience in critical decision-making.

Reagan quotes, "For an American of wisdom that honors the family, knowing that if the family goes, so goes our civilization . . . I thought the function of the government was to promote the general welfare, not to provide it."[180]

CHAPTER SIX

Educating Americans

America has been educating students for two hundred years, and it is still a work in progress. As we move into the twenty-first century, it is important to recognize that learning is a lifelong process from preschool through retirement. The world is changing rapidly, there is more to learn, and digital technology is changing the way we learn. Educators need to promote the importance and enjoyment of self-directed, lifelong learning, most of which will take place outside of the classroom. The nation's schools still have the responsibility for building the foundation of the learning process. The focus is no longer on imparting facts and knowledge, as that is readily accessible on the Internet. Educators saw these changes coming twenty years ago.[181]

We begin by examining the effectiveness of public education as measured by student-achievement outcomes. Again, the National Assessment of Educational Progress (NAEP) is the gold standard. Information gleaned from their reports over the past forty years is very reliable. Data is reported primarily in tabular format with breakdowns for grade levels by gender, race/ethnicity, parental education, and subject areas in each state.[182] In these pages, it will suffice to look at summative results, particularly for the last two testing intervals. Note that as of April 2016, the twelfth-grade results from 2015 have not yet been made public.

Examining the aggregate datas, in 2015, fourth-grade students had an average reading score of 223, and eighth-grade students had an average score of 265 (0- to 500-point scale). Scores at both grade levels were higher in 2015 than those from the earliest reading assessments in 1992. The 2015 data showed that 36 percent of the fourth-grade students and 34 percent of eighth-grade students performed at or above the proficient level in reading. These results are an aggregate of all students tested at each grade level.

Given that the 2015 data are complete and reliable, we can break down the above data by race/ethnicity subgroups with confidence.

2015 Reading Results

Subgroups	Percentage at or above Proficient Level	
	Grade 4	Grade 8
White	46%	44%
Black	18%	16%
Hispanic	21%	21%
Asian	57%	54%
Am. Indian / Ak. Native	21%	22%

Examining the aggregate data in mathematics, in 2015, fourth-grade students had an average mathematics score of 240 points, and eighth-grade students had an average score of 282 points

(0- to 500-point scale). Scores at both grade levels were higher in 2015 than those from the earliest mathematics assessments in 1990. The 2015 data showed that 40 percent of the fourth-grade students and 33 percent of eighth-grade students perform at or above the proficient level in mathematics.

2015 Mathematics Results

Subgroups	Percentage at or above Proficient Level	
	Grade 4	Grade 8
White	51%	43%
Black	19%	13%
Hispanic	26%	19%
Asian	65%	61%
Am. Indian / Ak. Native	23%	20%

It was noted that 2015 results for twelfth-grade students had not yet been reported. However, NAEP did a pilot study for twelfth-grade students in 2013. No conclusions or decisions should be based on the following synopsis because the data was derived from a pilot study. In reading, the 2013 results for twelfth-grade students decreased from the first assessment in 1992 and were essentially unchanged from the 2009 results. In mathematics, the 2013 results for twelfth-grade students increased from the 2005 results but were essentially unchanged from 2009 results. In terms of proficiency levels, 38 percent of twelfth-grade students were proficient in reading, and 26 percent were proficient in mathematics.

The Nation's Report Card is the only reliable ongoing assessment of what students know and can do in individual subjects. The following are based on assessments from 2010 to 2015.

Subject	Percentage at or above Proficient Level		
	Grade 4	Grade 8	Grade 12
Civics	27% in 2010	23% in 2014	24% in 2010
Economics	----- ☆	----- ☆	42% in 2012
Geography	21% in 2010	27% in 2014	20% in 2010
Mathematics	40% in 2015	33% in 2015	26% in 2013
Reading	36% in 2015	34% in 2015	38% in 2013
Science	----- ☆	32% in 2011	----- ☆
US History	20% in 2010	18% in 2014	12% in 2010
Writing	----- ☆	27% in 2011	27% in 2011

☆ Data not available.

The twelfth-grade student results reported immediately above were based on a pilot study. At the time, they were the best available data. However, in my final editing, I learned that NAEP had finally released the official twelfth-grade results. Herewith is a summation of these data.

In examining the overall reading achievement-level results, it can be seen that in 2015, thirty-seven percent of the twelfth-grade students performed at or above proficient on the reading assessment.

Overall Results Twelfth-Grade Reading Results

Year	Below Basic	Basic	Proficient	Advanced
2015	28%	35%	31%	6%
2009	26%	36%	33%	5%
2002	26%	38%	31%	5%
1998	23%	37%	35%	6%
1992	20%	39%	36%	4%

In 2015, twelfth-grade students had an average score of 287 on the NAEP 0-500 reading scale. This was not significantly different from the average score in 2013, but was lower in comparison to the earliest assessment in 1992.

2015 12th Grade Reading Results by Race/Ethnicity

Student group	Percentage at or above Proficient
White	46%
Black	17%
Hispanic	25%
Asian	49%
American Indian/Alaska Native	28%

The above results are self-explanatory. Approximately 18,700 twelfth-grade students completed the NAEP reading assessment in 2015. It is interesting to note that 49 percent of their parents had graduated from college.

Trend in 12th Grade Reading Achievement-Level Results by Race/Ethnicity (White Students)

Year	Below Basic	Basic	Proficient	Advanced
2015	21%	33%	38%	9%
2005	21%	36%	37%	6%
1998	18%	35%	40%	7%
1992	15%	38%	42%	5%

Trend in 12th Grade Reading Achievement-Level Results by Race/Ethnicity (Black Students)

Year	Below Basic	Basic	Proficient	Advanced
2015	48%	36%	15%	1%
2005	46%	38%	15%	1%
1998	43%	40%	16%	1%
1992	39%	43%	17%	1%

Trend in 12th Grade Reading Achievement-Level Results by Race/Ethnicity (Hispanic Students)

Year	Below Basic	Basic	Proficient	Advanced
2015	37%	38%	23%	2%

2005	40%	40%	18%	2%
1998	38%	38%	22%	2%
1992	33%	44%	22%	1%

Trend in 12th Grade Reading Achievement-Level Results by Race/Ethnicity (Asian/Pacific Islander)

Year	Below Basic	Basic	Proficient	Advanced
2015	21%	32%	38%	10%
2005	26%	38%	31%	5%
1998	26%	36%	33%	5%
1992	23%	37%	35%	5%

Trend in 12th Grade Reading Achievement-Level Results by Race/Ethnicity (American Indian/Alaska Native)

Year	Below Basic	Basic	Proficient	Advanced
2015	35%	36%	25%	3%
2005	33%	41%	24%	2%
1998	(insufficient sample size)			
1994	39%	41%	18%	2%

In examining the Overall mathematics achievement-level results, it can be seen that in 2015, twenty-five percent of the twelfth-grade students performed at or above proficient on the mathematics assessment.

Overall Results Twelfth-Grade Mathematics Results

Year	Below Basic	Basic	Proficient	Advanced
2015	38%	37%	22%	3%
2013	35%	39%	23%	3%
2009	36%	38%	23%	3%
2005	39%	38%	21%	2%

In 2015, twelfth-grade students had an average score of 152 on the NAEP 0-300 mathematics scale. This was lower compared to the average in 2013, but not significantly different in comparison to 2005.

2015 12th Grade Mathematics Results by Race/Ethnicity

Subgroups	Percentage at or above Proficient
White	32%
Black	7%
Hispanic	12%
Asian	47%
American Indian/Alaska Native	10%

The above results are self-explanatory, and disappointing. Black, Hispanic, and American Indian students are clearly underachieving in mathematics. Approximately 13,200 students completed the NAEP mathematics assessment in 2015. It is noted that in this mathematics assessment, 37 percent of their parents had graduated from college.

Trends in 12th Grade Mathematics Achievement-Level Results by Race/Ethnicity (White Student)

Year	Below Basic	Basic	Proficient	Advanced
2015	27%	41%	28%	3%
2009	25%	42%	30%	3%
2005	30%	41%	26%	3%

Trends in 12th Grade Mathematics Achievement-Level Results by Race/Ethnicity (Black Students)

Year	Below Basic	Basic	Proficient	Advanced
2015	64%	29%	7%	0*
2009	63%	30%	6%	0
2005	70%	25%	5%	0

*Rounds to zero

Trends in 12th Grade Mathematics Achievement-Level Results by Race/Ethnicity (Hispanic Students)

Year	Below Basic	Basic	Proficient	Advanced
2015	53%	35%	11%	1%
2009	55%	34%	11%	0*
2005	60%	32%	8%	0

*Rounds to zero

Trends in 12th Grade Mathematics Achievement-Level Results by Race/Ethnicity (Asian/Pacific Islander)

Year	Below Basic	Basic	Proficient	Advanced
2015	22%	32%	37%	9%
2009	16%	32%	41%	10%
2005	27%	37%	30%	6%

Trends in 12th Grade Mathematics Achievement-Level Results by Race/Ethnicity (American Indian/Alaska Native)

Year	Below Basic	Basic	Proficient	Advanced
2015	54%	36%	10%	0*

| 2009 | 44% | 45% | 11% | 0 |
| 2005 | 58% | 36% | 5% | 1% |

*Rounds to zero

The aggregate and subgroup student achievement data present factual evidence relative to the decline in American education. The statistics used in the analyses were appropriate and yield results in which readers can have a high level of confidence. NAEP stayed within statistical limits, for example, by not reporting results in categories where the sample size fell below the acceptable threshold. The results are very reliable and valid. Moreover, one can see the relative consistency of the data, particularly as it relates to the longitudinal performance results for the several racial/ethnic subgroups.

Readers are encouraged to go beyond the factual data, and surmise the reasons which may account for significant differences in student achievement among the subgroups. For example, is Asian student achievement a function of unique cultural differences? Are the Native American student achievement results related to the quality of education provided by the schools on Indian reservations, or is there a strong cultural component? We have no definitive answers to these questions. They do need to be answered in an objective and unbiased environment.

Examining the overall or aggregate data, we need to better understand why public education in America is in decline. Researchers ought to begin with a comprehensive factor-analysis of the likely variables impacting student achievement. This will be a formidable undertaking. Consider some of the likely factors: the proliferation of drugs, the ever present smart phone, time expended on social media, the increase in single parent families, employment issues, family financial stress. Are too many teachers not challenging students to compete and achieve at the highest level of their ability. Has education moved too far in the direction of affective development, rather than students' cognitive development? Are teachers overly concerned about how students feel, rather than how they are thinking?

We need research informed understanding of the relative impact of the factors that correlate with student achievement. We know that students on average are not performing up to their potential. Government has the money to fund the research. Is there a higher priority than the education of our children? Must we lose another generation?

For a more complete assessment of how well US students perform in an international comparison, this writer used data from the Program for International Student Assessment (PISA),[183] which was coordinated by the Organization for Economic Cooperation and Development (OECD). PISA assessed the competencies of fifteen-year-olds in reading, mathematics, and science in sixty-five countries. Approximately five hundred ten thousand students between the ages of fifteen years, three months and sixteen years, two months participated in PISA 2012.

PISA international results are reported by average scale score from theoretical zero to one thousand, as well as by percentages of students reaching particular proficiency levels. The following table reports the scale score as it was thought to be more meaningful than percentage scores. The table shows the country with the highest score, lowest score, and the average score for all countries.

PISA International Students		
Reading Literacy		
(Average: 496)	570	Shanghai, China
	498	United States
	384	Peru
Mathematics		
(Average: 494)	613	Shanghai, China
	481	United States
	368	Peru
Science Literacy		
(Average: 501)	580	Shanghai, China
	497	United States
	373	Peru

It can be seen that in reading, the US students scored slightly above the OECD average, and in science, the United States was slightly below the OECD average. In both of these subjects, the US scores were not statistically significantly different from the average score of all international students. In mathematics, the US score was significantly lower than the average score for all students.

The Nation's Report Card and the PISA student achievement assessment results are deeply disturbing. Too few students are functioning at high levels of proficiency. Fewer than half the students are proficient in reading. Even worse are the results for our minority populations, where fewer than one-fourth of the students are achieving proficiency in reading. A half century after *Brown v. Board of Education*, and schools are still not adequately preparing these students for higher education and careers, thereby limiting their opportunity for upward socioeconomic mobility. Later in this chapter, evidence will be presented that makes clear that our system of higher education is in decline. The federal Department of Education has enjoyed more than adequate funding and certainly has had enough time to enable the proper education for all of the nation's children.

Sadly, we knew that our nation's schools were not properly educating students more than thirty years ago when A Nation at Risk report was made public.[184] For example, the report noted that average Scholastic Aptitude Test scores dropped over fifty points in the verbal section and nearly forty points in mathematics between 1963 and 1980. It presented unfavorable comparisons with students in foreign countries. Readers can readily see that the results in 2015 are essentially the same as they were in 1980. Presidential Commissions on Education go back at least to the Truman administration; the most notable were the A Nation at Risk by President Reagan and Goals 2000 by President Clinton. The federal Department of Education has a long history of failures. In the private sector, no corporation will tolerate such an egregious pattern of failure, and the department will be abolished/ replaced within seven years.

The US Constitution leaves the responsibility for public K–12 education with the states.[185] It is recommended that the federal Department of Education be abolished and responsibility returned to the individual states. Congressional action will be required to disentangle the myriad of laws and regulations. It should be accomplished within seven years. Selected components should be moved into other departments. The Bureau of Statistics/ Assessment should remain at the federal level. Consideration should be given to moving the Office for Civil Rights to the Department of Justice. White House educational initiatives should be eliminated during the first three years of a new administration, including the following:

- White House Initiative on American Indian and Alaskan Native Education
- White House Initiative on Educational Excellence for Hispanics
- White House Initiative on Educational Excellence for African Americans
- White House Initiative on Asian Americans and Pacific Islanders
- White House Initiative on Historically Black Colleges and Universities

We are all Americans. Hyphenation does not serve our nation in the 21st century.[186]

The Center Faith-Based and Neighborhood Partnerships should be moved to the state level and function as a unit within state education departments.

There are several excellent Historically Black Colleges and Universities. They can be confident of receiving broad financial support from corporations, alumni/alumnae, charitable trusts, private foundations, and other organizations. In the twenty-first century, it is no longer in the nation's interest to use government monies to support Black colleges or Tribal colleges. Institutions that provide quality higher education will continue to do so; too many have not done so, and they will not fare well in the open marketplace.

Every state has a department of education. Individual counties and large cities have educational entities that are responsive to the states' education departments. The structures to accommodate the federal responsibilities are already in place. The transition will be challenging. Funding ought not to be an issue. The president's budget request for 2016 included $70.7 billion in discretionary appropriations for the Department of Education.[187] Looking at a more complete listing of funds, the federal government allocated approximately $154 billion on education in fiscal year 2015.[188] States are properly cautioned. Programs and services at the state level must be carefully designed at the state level so as to not become unmanageable/unaccountable. The Office of State Ombudsman (OSO) previously recommended will be the eyes and ears of the people at the state level and will have responsibility across all state functions.

There are two conditions that have a profound influence on the education of children: parenting, and substance abuse. Parents who read to their children when they are two and three years old and instill in them the value and enjoyment of reading give their children a significant advantage as they enter formal education. In an age of smartphones and social media, too often parents neglect this important responsibility. During these early formative years, children are better at learning language skills and reading as well as developing lifelong reading/learning habits. The role of the family unit and parenting should be promoted by schools and community, including churches. Formal preschool education should be an option for every family. Programs that include direct parent participation have been found to be the most effective.[189] They are the building blocks of formal education. Unfortunately, too often preschool programs are little more than babysitting centers, and this is counterproductive to child development and parenting. It is recommended that preschool education be a mandated responsibility of every school district. Enrollment of children will be a parental prerogative but should be promoted by schools and community organizations. The investment that we make in our children will yield lifelong benefits for society.[190] There are model programs in place that can be replicated in school districts across the country.

The second condition influencing the education of our children is substance abuse. A plethora of research studies documents the relationship between drug use and learning. Negative effects include shorter student attention span and memory and are reflected in poor attendance, declining achievement, and high school dropout rates.[191] This writer had the opportunity to operationalize his belief system relative to the debilitating effects of substance use when he was appointed district superintendent in an affluent school district.[192, 193] It can be accomplished, and the results are gratifying.

There has been a trend in education to promote a student's self-esteem by not emphasizing individual achievement and moving students away from competition.[194] A positive self-concept is important, but competition is a worthy strategy and can enhance a student's self-esteem. Students need to learn to compete, learn that at times, you win and often you do not. Making your best effort with one's given abilities is what really counts in life. It is an important lesson for students to experience within the comfort of a school environment.

Students appreciate structure, discipline, and clear objectives/expectations. Parental involvement in their child's education is an important element throughout the process. Students will achieve if they have had a good preschool experience, are in a school with a drug-free culture, and are administered by a strong principal. In that climate, teachers can engage as professional educators. In a digital environment, teaching methods should focus on personalized instruction and adaptive learning. However, homework is still important for the student, to facilitate parental involvement in their child's progress. It should be assigned regularly. The student's completed handwritten assignment should be returned promptly to each student, with the teachers' written comments. It is recognized that schools are transitioning to digital/ internet homework. The downside is that parents may not be as actively involved. Teachers should have adequate support personnel readily available for consultation. The student-counselor ratio should not exceed one counselor for 250 students, and the same counselor should remain with the same students as long as they are in the building.

Strong administrative leadership in every school building in the state is essential for setting the tone. With building principals being accountable for student achievement in their building, they must have a strong voice in the assignment of teachers and support personnel to their building. Building principals will be relieved of bureaucratic paperwork and have more time to move throughout their building, observing, interacting, and setting the tone.

Public education must be made uniformly transparent across each state. Schools should be judged, not students. And each school must be judged on the basis of students' achievement regardless of socioeconomic level. A base level of achievement should be in each student's record upon entrance into the educational program of a school building. There should be periodic assessments to reflect a student's educational progress. School-building aggregate student-achievement results should be mailed to every parent, along with their child's personal achievement results. Building principals will be held accountable for student achievement in their building.

Looking beyond the individual building and district level, attention is now directed at educational reform at the state level. There have been numerous reforms over the past three decades, many exemplary models developed, but it typically ends with a principal or superintendent receiving an award in Washington.[195] The exemplary models are rarely replicated. Administrators return to their school districts, and the federal department moves on with new initiatives. "The condition is serious, progressive in nature and can be fatal in terms of our ability to compete in the marketplace of the global economy in the next millennium."[196]

In a speech to school district superintendents, then governor Clinton stated, "Nearly every problem in American education has been solved by somebody, somewhere. What we can never seem to do is to figure out how to replicate it."[197] In 2016, we now have the requisite tools and financial resources, and with the federal government out of the picture, we can begin reforming education. There are only two major obstacles: overregulation and tenure. This writer attempted to opt out of tenure twice but was denied by law in New York and New Jersey.[198] Subsequently, I authored several articles advocating the abolition of tenure in public education.[199] While some progress has been made, tenure will be with us for another decade. But education's most sacred cow is dying. Every state should abolish tenure for all newly certified educators.

Unless one has been in the administrators' trenches for a few years, it is difficult to appreciate the impact of overregulation on education. It is the second obstacle to reforming education. It is less visible but almost as detrimental to educational reform as tenure. Government agencies regulate just about everything that the unions don't control. States have developed elaborate procedures to determine whether school districts are in compliance with all of the states' regulations and meeting state achievement standards. These periodic assessments are usually referred to as state monitoring, which is a very expensive and time-consuming process. Some districts hire special personnel or private consultants to shepherd the school district through the tedious process. This has the advantage of sparing teachers and supervisors from having to shortchange their regular duties with students. The disadvantage is that these consultants are rarely familiar with the school's functioning. They are very good at understanding the state's protocol for monitoring and how to demonstrate that the school district is in compliance.

This writer repeatedly urged the state to offer relief from the regulatory monitoring for those school districts that have a history of being among the top 5 percent of districts in the state, especially those districts/schools that have been recognized nationally for their exemplary programs and high level of student achievement.[200] Relief from the time-consuming documentation process would permit high-performing districts to allocate their time and financial and personnel resources in a manner consistent with their high level of prior achievement. Regulatory relief would also be an incentive for other school districts so that they too would be relieved of what most school districts have found to be an educationally counterproductive ritual. States should consider regulatory relief that balances flexible compliance with school district accountability.

Charter schools are typically free of the state regulatory environment. Some maintain that this freedom is partially responsible for the rapid growth of the Charter School Movement. The number of charter schools surpassed six thousand at the start of the 2012–2013 school year, as these schools, which are publicly financed but privately run, steadily increased by 7 percent throughout the United States that year.[201] California enrolled the largest number of students in charter schools (471,000) representing 8 percent of the total public school students in the state. As of 2013, Arizona had 14 percent of their total public school population enrolled in charter schools.[202] This writer participated in developing high-quality, community-based education almost fifty years ago and observed the power of parents in designing schools to meet the needs of their children.[203] Community-based charter schools are expanding rapidly for good reason. Many of these schools provide a better education and require less funding than traditional schools.

Examining recent New York City student achievement data, the Wall Street Journal noted that student proficiency increased this year on average by 7.6 percentage points in English and 1.2 percentage points in mathematics. Thus the proficiency level in English was 38% and in mathematics it was 36%. Yet strikingly, proficiency in the City's charter schools this year jumped 13.7 percentage points in English and 4.5 percentage points in mathematics resulting in proficiency levels of 43% and 47%, respectively!

Further, a recent analysis by Families for Excellent Schools found that New York City charter schools, whose student populations are more than 90% Black and Hispanic, raised their local community school district proficiency rates by 13%. Black and Hispanic students who attended charter schools scored 73% higher than their counterparts at district-run schools.

These astounding outcomes beg the question: what can traditional public schools learn from charter schools about how best to educate minority students. Charter schools provide an excellent educational alternative, particularly for our minority students.

Just as the unions (American Federation of Teachers and National Education Association) resist tenure and the charter school movement, they have contributed to the controversy surrounding Common Core.[204] This important education reform has become too politicized. Parents are confused; states are reversing or modifying their initial support. Much of the resistance to the Common Core Standards (CSS) has actually been resistance against the federal government usurping the right of the state over education.[205] Eliminating the federal education department will remove that obstacle. CCS has developed excellent uniform standards and establishes clear achievement expectations for students. These standards are geared toward both college and career readiness, as well as competition in the global economy. They deserve to be implemented. Individual states need not adopt the entire CCS program. There is provision whereby states can make modifications to meet unique needs of their student populations.

Public education's structure is comprised of more than 13,000 independent school districts. While there has been considerable centralization during the past two decades, further consolidation can, and should be accomplished. There is typically strong and vehement opposition to consolidating school districts. However, the educational and financial advantages have been well documented.[206]

America's colleges and universities have been in decline for the past three decades. A college education costs too much and delivers too little. Students are graduating with too much student loan debt, but without much evidence that they grew in either knowledge or critical thinking, stated the president of Purdue University.[207] It is disheartening to know that 45 percent of college graduates are returning to live with their parents.[208] Approximately, 50 percent of these graduates take five to seven years to complete degree requirements. Many believe that this degree is the equivalent of a high school diploma from a quality high school. Often these college graduates are unable to find a job and are unwilling to work in a fast-food restaurant. This makes for an uncomfortable condition in the family home.

The average 2015 college graduate with student loan debt will have to pay back more than $35,000.[209] As of April 2016, student loan debt was $1,402,944,782,355.[210] By the time you read this, student loan debt will be more than $1.5 trillion. President Obama is encouraging loan recipients to claim that they were misled by colleges. The Department of Education recently expedited closed-school discharge claims from forty thousand students at Corinthian's Heald College (an accredited college). The department estimated that eighty-five thousand additional Corinthian students may be eligible for loan relief. Department data show that the first 5,814 claims approved for former Corinthian students came to about seventy-five million dollars. If eighty-five thousand more students are granted relief, taxpayers may face a bill for over one billion dollars for this institution alone.[211] Current student debt is $1.4 trillion, and the bubble continues to grow larger. Why were these colleges granted accreditation? Student loan forgiveness is never a good incentive for other college graduates to pay off their loans. Are we teaching these graduates that their future mortgage loans may also be forgiven? It is recommended that the entire federal student loan program be abolished. This will result in a proliferation of private lending institutions. Students will be charged higher interest rates, and they will understand that these loans will not be forgiven.

There are many families that cannot afford to send their children to college. For them, the federal Pell Grant program should remain in place. However, recipients of these grants should be required to work on campus. One can recall a time when students could actually work their way through college.[212]

At the college level, it is proposed that all diversity quotas, mandates, and initiatives be rescinded/abolished. Approaching 2017, they are no longer necessary or even desirable. Preferential advantage on the basis of race, ethnicity, or gender is counterproductive.[213]

This writer has been involved in the education of minority youth for more than half a century. In April 1970, I wrote an editorial entitled "In Support of Recruiting Negroes,"[214] which was in response to the *Pocono Record*, March 25, 1970, editorial entitled "Recruiting Wrong." The main point was that it would be wrong to admit Negroes into colleges where most would experience failure because they were ill-prepared for the rigors of academia. Many of the colleges had a hidden agenda, which was to bolster their athletic teams. Too many educationally disadvantaged minority youth were admitted to college under open enrollment, experienced academic failure, and dropped out with a weakened sense of self.

I wrote, "Your Editorial is indicative of a gross insensitivity to the plight of minority groups, and a total ignorance of the social, political, and economic complexities involved in providing minority group members an equal educational collegiate opportunity." Even Lyndon B. Johnson was sufficiently perceptive to recognize this fallacy when he said, "You do not take a person who has been hobbled by chains and liberate him, bring him up to the starting line of a race and say, 'You're free to compete with the others,' and justly believe that you have been completely fair."

The evidence, I wrote, "was irrefutable that until each American has full access to the means to develop his capacities, every other American's chances and attainments will continue to be diminished."

At this point in the twenty-first century, there are adequate laws to protect the rights of special groups. It is imperative that antidiscrimination laws be rigorously enforced.[215] Whether violations occur in higher education, employment, or housing, the penalties must be severe.

The open marketplace is the ideal mechanism for filtering out the weak and giving rise to the best ideas, best products, and best services. People will decide what they will buy, whether it is in business or academia. Colleges offering high-quality education at market-driven cost will prosper. Our colleges and universities will self-correct and reform the academy. There will always be a place for the liberal arts in our colleges and universities. And there are many high-quality, nontraditional colleges and institutes that should be encouraged and not grouped together with the Corinthian-like colleges. For example, Monroe College and the DeVry Education Group have provided quality education and career training to hundreds of thousands of high school graduates over the past eighty years.

Accreditation in its current condition is neither necessary nor sufficient. If it is to serve a useful function, it must be completely restructured. The present system is functionally flawed. Fix it, or eliminate it.

Colleges may take a few pages from corporate America. Private offices with windows and corner views were cast aside in the business world decades ago, likely going back to Andy Grove's leadership at Intel. It will not be easy.[216]

Colleges need to violate the mystique of the university by becoming more transparent. One starting point will be to make admissions data, grade distribution data by department, and student job placement data by department readily available to prospective students and their parents. Curricula will be shaped as new specialties evolve.

Colleges need to rethink the role of adjunct faculty. The recent rapid growth in the number of adjunct instructors suggests that too often, they are employed for economic reasons rather than for their expertise. It is recommended that adjunct faculty be compensated more in line with the professoriat.

We need to remove the gray area between high school graduation and entry into the world of work. It should not be so difficult for young people to understand their options. We need to reconceptualize the manner in which we typically view postsecondary education by broadening the scope and legitimizing all paths into the world of work. Students and their parents should know about the array of choices, including community colleges, polytechnic institutes, military service, career-development programs, apprenticeships, and university education. Social value ought not to be attached to any option that enables high school graduates to set themselves on an educational path that best matches their unique set of aptitudes and interests and facilitates their movement into a fulfilling life as contributing members of society.

Community colleges will increasingly become the stepping stone into one's future. The community college may be the terminal degree, or it may be the bridge to further academic advancement. Community colleges should continue to broaden their offerings to include new technical certificate and degree programs. Specializations with promising career paths include software development, aesthetics, media technology, security, and numerous health care options. Community colleges should strengthen their partnerships with regional employers, including internships and related transitional programs. It is recommended that a community college education be cost-free for every high school graduate who satisfies the eligibility requirements for admission.

CHAPTER SEVEN

Action Guide to Transition America

The recommendations and proposals put forth in this final chapter should be thought of as guidance. This writer is providing specific direction regarding actions that are likely to be necessary in order to remediate the many ills plaguing this once-great nation in order to bring it in line with its constitutional mission to protect, defend, and serve the people. Obviously, there must be appropriate give-and-take to provide experienced professionals who have specific expertise-adequate flexibility. It is they who have the burden of responsibility for implementing the necessary reforms to enable the federal government to get back on the track that it was on in the aftermath of World War II.

Three of the following recommendations call for the next president to issue executive orders. It must be made clear that the June 2016 Supreme Court ruling on President Obama's use of this power was limited to his executive order on undocumented immigrants. In a 4 to 4 tie, the Supreme Court was deadlocked on the president's order to shield as many as five million undocumented immigrants from deportation, and allow them to work legally in the United States. The Supreme Court's action left in place an appeals court ruling which blocked the president's plan.

Almost every president has issued executive orders. Not all of these orders were for the public good. President Obama's order abused this power, as it was not in the best interest of American citizens. This author's proposals to limit the C.I.A.'s use of weaponized drones, and to increase the pay grades for our military personnel are certainly for the public good.

1. It is proposed that the United States close selected embassies and diplomatic posts in the Middle East, Asia, and Africa (for a beginning list of facilities in nineteen countries, see chapter 2 text).

2. It is recommended that all US financial aid to foreign countries and military weapons aid to foreign countries be entirely phased out by 2023.

3. It is recommended that the water reservoirs and power grids serving metropolitan areas in the United States be secured by professional personnel under the direction of the Department of Homeland Security.

4. It is proposed that Presidential Policy Directive 28 be rescinded and that the directive be rewritten to delete the privacy rights of non-US citizens and the onerous requirements to justify data collection.

5. It is recommended that the next president issue an executive order that places a ban on the CIA's use of weaponized drones and limits the CIA's use of drones to data collection.

6. It is recommended that Enforcement and Removal Operation (ICE: ERO) personnel be directed to discontinue the proactive practice of providing access to

legal resources and representatives of advocacy groups to identified removable aliens.

7. It is strongly recommended that illegal aliens with a criminal conviction be deported immediately.

8. It is proposed that Congress enact legislation that denies federal funds to sanctuary cities as violators of the Illegal Immigration Reform and Immigrant Responsibility Act of 1996.

9. By executive order, the president will place a freeze on immigration for an indefinite period of time, with provision for limited extreme-hardship visas under the supervision of a DHS unit.

10. It is proposed that Congress enact legislation authorizing the US Army Corps of Engineers (USACE) to construct an impenetrable/untunnelable wall along the entire length of the US-Mexican border.

11. By act of Congress, the US Border Patrol be directed to order (in English and Spanish) any individual attempting to illegally enter the United States to stop and reverse direction and further contain the authority to shoot those who refuse to obey the command.

12. It is recommended that the US Border Patrol deploy twenty thousand agents along the Canadian border and reduce the number of agents on the Mexican border to ten thousand.

13. By act of Congress, the Diversity Visa Program should be abolished immediately.

14. An entering immigrant identified as high-risk will have a tracking chip implanted, which, if deactivated, will signal an ICE alert for arrest and deportation.

15. It is recommended that law-abiding, unauthorized immigrants residing within the United States be made eligible for American citizenship.

16. It is strongly recommended that Congress approve the Cyber Act of War of 2016 (S.2905) and that the president sign it into law.

17. It is recommended that the United States begin immediately to transition all American military forces out of Korea, Japan, and Vietnam.

18. It is recommended that the Pentagon be ordered to remove all military personnel from the African continent.

19. It is recommended that all military personnel be transitioned from the Middle East and redeployed stateside.

20. It is recommended that the United States nullify its NATO membership.

21. It is recommended that the Pentagon be ordered to abort the Terminal High Altitude Area Defense system for South Korea and reallocate that funding to the Missile Defense Agency to expedite the Long-Range Discrimination Radar system by 2020.

22. It is recommended that by congressional action, the Pentagon's civilian personnel force be reduced in size 25 percent by December 31, 2018.

23. By presidential order, military pay grades E-1 through E-9 and W-1 through W-5 are to be raised 5 percent effective October 1, 2018.

24. By presidential order, military pay grades 0-6 through 0-11 are to be raised 9.5 percent effective October 1, 2018.

25. It is strongly recommended that the president rescind Executive Order No. 13491: Ensuring Lawful Interrogations.

26. It is strongly recommended that Congress amend the Constitution requiring an annual balanced budget with no loopholes.

27. It is strongly recommended that Congress enact legislation that changes the length of a term for members of the House of Representatives to four years and lengthen the Senate term to seven years.

28. It is proposed that states be required to create an Office of State Ombudsman to include a special unit protecting the rights of whistle-blowers.

29. It is recommended that the president rescind Executive Order No. 13592: Tribal Colleges.

30. By presidential order, the White House Initiatives on American Indians, Hispanics, African Americans, and Asian Americans should be rescinded.

31. It is strongly recommended that the Bureau of Indian Affairs be abolished.

32. It is proposed that a nongovernmental entity, such as Booz Allen Hamilton in McLean, Virginia (or comparable firm), be contracted to make recommendations to reduce the number of federal agencies by 50 percent and to reduce the size of the remaining agencies by 50 percent.

33. It is proposed that the regular average social security benefit be increased 3 percent by January 1, 2018.

34. It is proposed that the cap on taxable social security earnings be raised from the current $118,500 to as follows: $120,000 in 2018, $122,000 in 2020, $125,000 in 2023, and $129,000 in 2027.

35. It is proposed that the eligibility age to receive early social security benefits be raised to age sixty-five by 2028, as delineated in the text.

36. It is proposed that the eligibility age to receive full social security benefits be raised to age seventy in gradations, as delineated in the text.

37. It is proposed that Congress enact a financial incentive for individuals who choose to work beyond the age at which they would be entitled to full social security benefits.

38. It is strongly recommended that a simple flat 10 percent income tax rate be enacted by Congress for everybody who has income.

39. It is proposed that Congress enact legislation that exempts earned interest from taxation and sets the tax rate on capital gains and dividends at 10 percent.

40. It is strongly recommended that Congress enact legislation to establish a 3 to 5 percent federal sales tax, with provision to exempt food and medicine.

41. It is proposed that Congress enact legislation that changes the corporate tax rate to an average rate of 16 percent, with a range from 12 percent to 19 percent.

42. It is proposed that an independent body be commissioned to evaluate the strategies and loopholes that corporations have been using and make appropriate recommendations.

43. Under the proposed tax model, the Internal Revenue Service personnel should be reduced from the current 82,203 employees to approximately one thousand employees.

44. Given the adoption of the previous recommendation, the IRS should be transferred as a unit to the Department of Treasury.

45. It is proposed that the Gary Horlick law firm (or comparable competent firm in the Washington area) be engaged to guide the United States out of multilateral trade agreements.

46. It is proposed that Congress enact legislation to provide dedicated block grants to individual states to facilitate and subsidize the construction and development of manufacturing facilities.

47. It is strongly recommended that Congress enact legislation to rescind the October 19, 1960, Cuban Trade Embargo as well as each of the subsequent acts that strengthened the embargo.

48. It is strongly recommended that Puerto Rico not be bailed out and not be granted financial relief. Statehood should be encouraged.

49. It is strongly recommended that Congress enact legislation creating a Work America Relief (WAR) program, as detailed in chapter 5.

50. It is strongly recommended that Congress enact legislation that raises the federal minimum wage to nine dollars per hour in 2018 and increase it by one dollar until a minimum hourly wage of fifteen dollars is in place in 2024.

51. It is proposed that the nongovernmental entity Bozz Allen Hamilton (or comparable firm) be contracted to conduct an assessment of the Department of Veterans Affairs and make detailed recommendations for VA restructuring.

52. It is recommended that Veterans Affairs officials be directed to facilitate the transition of returning veterans into the workforce and job-training programs.

53. It is strongly recommended that all antipoverty programs be phased out over a period of time ending in 2025.

54. It is proposed that Congress enact legislation that abolishes and phases out the Affordable Care Act over a period of five years.

55. It is proposed that Congress enact legislation that requires and enables states to develop local and regional Available Health-Welfare Centers (AHWC) with funding in the form of federal block grants to every state.

56. It is proposed that the Center Faith-Based and Neighborhood Partnerships initiative be moved to the state level.

57. It is strongly recommended that early childhood education be mandated by states as a requirement of all school districts whereby children 3.5 years of age will be eligible for enrollment as a parental prerogative.

58. It is strongly recommended that all federal student loan programs be abolished by congressional action.

59. It is strongly recommended that all diversity-quota initiatives in state colleges and universities be rescinded/abolished.

60. It is strongly recommended that community college education be cost-free for every high school graduate who satisfies the requirements for admission.

61. It is strongly recommended that a grassroots People's Party be established by the people and for the people with the dedicated mission of transitioning America by radically reducing the size of the federal government and reforming the essential residual components.

Throughout this book, attention has been focused on the future of America. Most of the foregoing recommendations will require strong presidential leadership and a motivated and supportive congress. There is scant evidence on the horizon to suggest that these two conditions will prevail. Tinkering about in piecemeal manner will be both insufficient and counterproductive, in which case the nuclear option, Article 5, will need to be activated. It is proposed that a grassroots People's Party be established by the people and for the people with the dedicated mission of transitioning America by radically reducing the size of federal government and reforming the essential residual components. Just do it.

Quoting President Reagan, "Either you will control your government, or government will control you."[217] A People's Party movement should consider Article 5 of the US Constitution as an overriding vehicle. It reads, "The Congress, whenever two thirds of both Houses shall deem it necessary, shall propose amendments to this Constitution, Or, on the application of the legislatures of two thirds of the several states, shall call a convention for proposing amendments, which, in either case, shall be valid to all intents and purposes, as part of this Constitution, when ratified by the legislatures of three fourths of the several states, or by conventions in three fourths thereof, as the one or the other mode of ratification may be proposed by the Congress."[218] The writers of our Constitution, the architects of our federal government, had the foresight to make provision, within the pages of the Constitution, for the protection of its people from the federal government, should that condition ever prevail. As evidenced in the selection of candidates for president and our dysfunctional federal government, we, the people, may suffer that condition.

EPILOGUE

This writing began as a letter to a local newspaper editor and became a book. I began with very few preconceived formulations. I do have knowledge and experience with poverty, the education/empowerment of minority group members, and enabling forgotten subsets of Americans. My first publication in 1962 was entitled *Helping the Forgotten Students in our Schools*[219] and, years later, *Gerontological Counseling and Developing Socially and Psychologically Supportive Environments for the Aged.*[220]

As I began writing, I formulated tentative conclusions with respect to our foreign policy, terrorism, military direction and the economy. Subsequently, I formed the definitive conclusion that the root cause of most problems facing America is the failure of our oversize federal government.

Absent a groundswell movement, the oversized bureaucracy of agencies, departments, institutes, and initiatives will continue in a dysfunctional manner, growing still larger and unresponsive to the needs of the people. The president will continue to lead by executive fiat, creating laws, ignoring the Constitution, and weakening the Supreme Court. US military aggression abroad will continue causing the radicalization of more young people, and the perpetuation of pervasive terrorist attacks within the United States.

The federal government must stop meddling in Americans' lives, redistributing the personal wealth of individuals, and attempting to democratize sovereign states. Given the gravity of America's condition, we need to elect strong government people at all levels of government—*strong*, because those who do not fall in line with the majority rule are typically marginalized, embarrassed, kept off important committees, and often shunned.

The time is now for Americans to think, to talk, and to act. Talk with your neighbor, colleague, and preacher. All registered voters need to get the vote out. We, the people, must begin now to take America back before it is too far gone. Power to the People's Party.

All profits derived from this Xlibris book will be donated to People for the Ethical Treatment of Animals and the Paralyzed Veterans of America.

US senator Bill Bradley congratulates the author.

Appendix A

Growth of the US National Debt

Year	National Debt	President
1796	$83,762,172	George Washington
1864	$1,815,784,370	Abraham Lincoln
1908	$2,626,806,271	Theodore Roosevelt
1944	$201,003,387,221	Franklin D. Roosevelt
1960	$286,330,760,848	Dwight D. Eisenhower
1968	$347,578,406,425	Lyndon B. Johnson
1988	$2,602,337,712,041	Ronald Reagan
1995	$4,973,982,900,709	William J. Clinton
2000	$5,674,178,209,886	William J. Clinton
2005	$7,932,709,661,723	George W. Bush
2010	$13,561,623,030,891	Barack Obama
2015	$18,825,061,664,535	Barack Obama
2016	$19,442,913,162,409	Barack Obama

Appendix B-1

Aid to Foreign Countries in America Dollars

Continent	Country	2012	2013
Asia	Afghanistan	$6,725,000,000	$5,265,950,000
Africa	Algeria	$144,500,000	$207,960,000
Asia	Bangladesh	$2,152,000,000	$2,669,100,000
Americas	Bolivia	$658,600,000	$699,150,000
Africa	Burkina Faso	$1,158,500,000	$1,040,110,000
Asia	Cambodia	$807,400,000	$804,810,000
Africa	Cameroon	$596,200,000	$737,49,000
Africa	Chad	$478,500,000	$399,330,000
Americas	Columbia	$764,400,000	$852,030,000
Africa	Congo, Dem. Rep.	$2,859,300,000	$2,572,200,000
Africa	Ethiopia	$3,261,300,000	$3,826,200,000
Europe	Georgia	$662,200,000	$652,700,000
Africa	Ghana	$1,807,900,000	$1,330,500,000

Americas	Haiti	$1,275,100,000	$1,170,500,000
Asia	India	$1,667,630,000	$2,435,680,000
Middle East	Iraq	$1,300,700,000	$1,541,400,000
Middle East	Israel	$3,070,000,000	$3,150,000,000
Middle East	Jordan	$1,416,900,000	$1,407,900,000
Africa	Kenya	$2,654,000,000	$3,236,200,000
Middle East	Lebanon	$710,000,000	$626,400,000
Africa	Malawi	$1,174,600,000	$1,125,800,000
Africa	Mali	$1,001,300,000	$1,391,300,000
Africa	Morocco	$1,480,300,000	$1,966,100,000
Africa	Mozambique	$2,096,900,000	$2,314,100,000
Africa	Nigeria	$1,915,800,000	$2,529,400,000
Africa	Senegal	$1,080,100,000	$982,800,000
Asia	Pakistan	$3,109,000,000	$2,174,100,000
Europe	Serbia	$1,089,800,000	$783,200,000
Africa	Somalia	$998,600,000	$991,900,000
Africa	South Africa	$1,067,100,000	$1,292,900,000
Africa	South Sudan	$1,578,000,000	$1,447,400,000
Africa	Sudan	$983,200,000	$1,163,100,000
Middle East	Syria	$1,671,500,000	$3,626,700,000
Africa	Tanzania	$2,831,800,000	$3,430,200,000
Africa	Tunisia	$1,017,000,000	$713,600,000
Asia	Turkey	$3,033,100,000	$2,740,500,000
Africa	Uganda	$1,655,100,000	$1,692,500,000

Asia	Vietnam	$4,115,700,000	$4,084,700,000
Middle East	Yemen	$709,300,000	$1,003,500,000
Africa	Zambia	$957,700,000	$1,142,400,000

Source: https://en.m.Wikipedia.org/wiki/list_of_Foreign_Aid _Recipients

APPENDIX B-2

Aid to Foreign Countries: FY 2014

Countries	Economic & Military aid
Afganistan	$ 7,244,140,000
Israel	$ 3,123,400,000
Jordan	$ 1,136,840,000
Pakistan	$ 980,870,000
Kenya	$ 891,670,000
South Sudan	$ 867,790,000
Syria	$ 795,440,000
Ethiopia	$ 742,170,000
Zambia	$ 672,900,000
Nigeria	$ 593,040,000
Tanzania	$ 589,370,000
Columbia	$ 560,390,000
Uganda	$ 557,270,000
S. Africa	$ 515,580,000
W. Bank/Gaza	$ 497,270,000
Congo	$ 438,560,000
Lebanon	$ 433,850,000

Iraq	$	410,180,000
Somalia	$	402,200,000
Haiti	$	355,290,000
Mozambique	$	337,120,000

Source: https://en.m.wikipedia.org/wiki/United_States_foreign _aid#recipients.

Appendix C

Candidate Stateside Military Bases for Redeployed
Special Military Personnel

Edwards AFB (CA)
Goldwater AFB (AZ)
Lewis-McChord (WA)
Elmendorf-Richardson (AK)
Ft. Campbell (KY/TN)
Cheyenne Mt. Complex (CO)
Wright-Patterson AFB (OH)
NAS Fallon Navy Base (NV)
Surface Forces Logistics CGB (MD)
Selfridge ANGB AFB (MI)
Warren AFB (WY)
Navigation CGB (VA)
Ft. Benning Army Base (GA)

Clearwater CGB (FL)
Ft. Bragg (NC)
Schofield Barracks (HI)
Ft. Benning (GA)
Shaw AFB (SC)
Palmdale Facility CA)
Eglin AFB (FL)
Arnold AFB (TN)
Junean CGB (AK)
Altus AFB (OK)
Berryville Facility (VA)
Luke AFB (AZ)
Ft. Bliss (TX)

Note: offshore facilities include the Guantanamo Naval Base and
the Naval Force Maria NAS Navy Base on Guam.

Appendix D

Agencies to Be Reduced

Agencies	2013 $ Outlays*			Employees
	Discretionary	Mandatory	Total	
Dept. of Agriculture	$26.8 Billion	$127.7 Billion	$154.5 Billion	105,000
Dept. of Defense	$666 Billion	$6.7 Billion	$672.9 Billion	742,000** (civilian employees)
Dept. of Housing and Urban Development	$41.1 Billion	$5.2 Billion	$46.3 Billion	8,416
Dept. of Health and Human Services	$440.9 Billion	$500 Billion	$940.9 Billion	79,540
Dept. of Education	$50.2 Billion	$4.2 Billion	$71.9 Billion	5,300
Dept. Veterans Affairs	$60.4 Billion	$79.4 Billion	$139.7 Billion	312,841

Environmental Protection Agency	$9.2 Billion	$-0.2 Billion	$8.9 Billion	15,913
Social Security Administration	$11.7 Billion	$871 Billion	$882.7 Billion	60,000

* h t t p s : / / e n . w i k i p e d i a . o r g / wiki/2013_United_States_federal_budget

**consideration should be given to replacing 200,000 civilian employees with military personnel

Note: Proposed reductions in the above agencies will make funds available to increase funding in D.H.S. and National Intelligence Program

Endnotes

Introduction

1   http://www.usgovernmentdebt.us/.

2   Paul Bedard, *Washington Examiner* (December 2014), http://www.washingtonexaminer.com/report-21000-regulations-so-far-under-obama-2375-set-for2015/article/2558050.

    Related: The Code of Federal Regulations contained 175,496 pages at year-end 2013, including a 1,170-page index.

    Clyde Wayne Crews, "New Data: Code of Federal Regulations Expanding Faster Under Obama," Competitive Enterprise Institute, March 17, 2014.

3   https://www.opm.gov/policy-data-oversight/data-analysis-documentation/federal-employment-reports/historical-tables/total-government-employment-since-1962/.

4   http://www.wsj.com/articles/missing/-u-s-missile-shows-up-in-cuba-1452213667.

5   https://www.washingtonpost.com/news/wonk/wp/2016/01/05/gun-sales-hit-new-record-ahead-of-new-obama-gun-restrictions/.

6   Note: my undergraduate degree was in mathematics, physics, and chemistry; my advanced degrees were in psychological counseling.

Chapter One
America in Decline

7   http://www.cnbc.com/2016/02/08/how-badly-will-boj-negative-rates-hit-japanese-megabank-earnings-analysts-views-differ.html.

8   http://www.brillig.com/debt_clock/.

9   Chris Edwards, "Pork: A Microcosm of the Overspending Problem," *Tax and Budget Bulletin* 24 (August 2005).
Related: Jacoby, *Boston Globe*, www.boston.com/news/globe/editorial-opinion/oped/2005/08/04/the-republican-pork-barrel.

10   http://www.AZQuotes.com/Quotes/topics/centralized-government.html.

11   Note: The writer developed a graduate course of study that focused on these consequences.
See: Teachers College Bulletin, Columbia University, Series 65, April 1974, p. 144.
TG 4111 Educational and Vocational Implications of Ethnic and Social Status Differences Description: Review of differential characteristics of subgroup members based on economic, ethnic, and social status in relation to educational and vocational opportunities. Implications for educational and career development.

12   http://en.m.wikipedia.org/wiki/hegemony.

13   Simon Reich and Richard Ned Lebow, *Good-Bye Hegemony: Power and Influence in the Global System* (Princeton: Princeton University Press, 2014).

14   Charles Krauthammer, "Decline Is a Choice: The New Liberalism and the End of American Ascendancy," *The Weekly Standard* (October 2009), http://www.weeklystandard.com/article/270813.

Chapter Two
Global Turmoil and America's Role

15   Alastair Gale, "North Korea Says It Made Advance on Warheads,"

Wall Street Journal, March 8, 2016.

16 http://www.ifamericaknew.org/history/.

17 http://m.mdtv.com/india-news/india-pakistan-foreign-secretary-talks-for-next-week-unlikely-1263213.

18 http://www.bbc.com/news/world-middle-east-35561845.

19 Andrea Thomas, "Germany Took in 1.1 Million Migrants in 2015," *Wall Street Journal* (January 2016): A8.
   Related: Serhii Plokhy, *The Gates of Europe* (New York: Basic Books, 2015).

20 Henry Kissinger, *World Order* (New York: Penguin Press, 2014), 108 and 114.

21 Paula A. Winters and David Benda and Bruce Leone, ed., *Islam Opposing Viewpoints* (San Diego: Greenhaven Press, 1995).
   Michael Jansen, *Terrorism Is a Response to Western Hypocrisy*, 167.

22 Ibid., 165.

23 Ibid., 164.

24 nsa archive.gwu.edu /nsaebb/nsaebb435/.
   Malcolm Byrne, "C.I.A. Confirms Role in Iran Coup: Agency Finally Owns Up to Its Role in the 1953 Operation TPAJAX" (the CIA's code name for the plot).

25 http://www.foreignaffairs.com/reviews/capsule-review /1996-03-01/secret-war-middle-east-covert-struggle-syria -1949-1961.

26 Andrew Rathmell, *Secret War in the Middle East: the Covert Struggle for Syria, 1949–1961* (London: IB Tauris, 1995).

27 J. Dana Stuster, http://www.foreignpolicy.com/2013/08/20mapped -the-7-governments-the-u-s-has-overthrown/.

28 Edward F. Mickolus, *Terrorism 1996–2001*, Vols. 1 and 2 (Westport: Glenwood Press, 2002), 559.

29 http://nsaarchive.gwu.edu/nsaebb/nsaebb8/nsaebb8i.htm.

30 Christopher A. Preble, www.nationalinterest.org/blog/ the-skeptics/who-will-shake-theforeign-policy-status-quo-14930 (accessed January 16, 2016).

Dr. Preble is the vice president for defense and foreign policy at the Cato Institute.

31   Salvatore Babones, http://www.nationalinterest.org/feature/American-hegemony-here-to-stay-13089.

32   Charles Krauthammer, "Decline Is a Choice: the New Liberalism and the End of American Ascendancy," *The Weekly Standard*, October 19, 2009.
http://www.weeklystandard.com/article/270813.
Christopher Layne, "The Waning of U.S. Hegemony: Myth or Reality? A Review Essay," *International Security* 34, no. 1: 147–172.
Barry R. Posen, "Command of the Commons: The Military Foundation of U.S. Hegemony," *International Security* 28, 1 (Summer 2003): 5–46

33   http://www.thediplomat.com/2013/09/do-we-still-need-embassies/.

34   http://www.theguardian.com/2013/dec/30/globalized-world-foreign-office-outlined-usefullness.

35   http://www.state.gov/r/pa/prs/ps/2011/12/178343.htm.

36   http://www.state.gov/documents/organization/213137.pdf.

37   http://www.foreignassistance.gov.

38   http://www.theguardian.com/business/economics-blog/2012/Apr/4/overseas-aid-golden-age-over.

39   https://www.washingtonpost.com/pentagon-spent-$43million-on-a-single-gas-station.

40   William Easterly, *The White Man's Burden: Why the West's Efforts to Aid the Rest Have Done So Much Ill and so Little Good* (Penguin Press, 2006), 4.

41   http://vocativ.com/usa/us-politics/irony-alert-u-s-gives-aid-countries-hate-us/.

42   http://www.pewglobal.org.

43   www.infrastructure report card.org/grades/

44   http://www.beta.foreignassistance.gov.

45   http://www.state.gov/documents/organization/238223.pdf.

46 www.pepfar.gov/funding/budget/index.

Note: Readers may be interested in *War and Peace in the Law of Islam* by Majid Khadduri (Baltimore: John Hopkins Press, 1995). This classic was reprinted in 2006 and 2010 by Lawbook Exchange Ltd.

Chapter Three
Managing Terrorism and Our National Security

47 John C. Miller, Michael Stone, and Christ Mitchell, *The Cell: Inside the 9/11 Plot, and Why the FBI and CIA Failed to Stop It* (New York: Hachette Books, 2002).

48 http://pmakakul.blogspot.com/.

49 http://en.m.wikipedia.org/wiki/2009_Fort_Hood_shooting.

50 http://www.foxnews.com/story/2009/11/12/hasan-called-himself-soldier-allah-on-business-cards.htm.

51 Kathy Gilsinan, "Counting the ISIS Dead," *The Atlantic*, October 15, 2015.

(also) http://www.theatlantic.com/internationalarchive/2015/10/us-isis-fighters-killed/410599.

52 Melissa Clyne, "Gen. Dempsey: ISIS Cannot Be Defeated without Going into Syria," *Newsmax*, August 22, 2014.

http://www.newsmax.com/+/newsmax/article/590253.

53 Nathan Hodge, "In Tajikistan, U.S.-Trained Commander Turns to Islamic State," *Wall Street Journal*, January 4, 2016, A-5.

54 http://www.wikipedia.org/wiki/soviet-afghan_war#january_1987_e2.80.93_february_1989_withdrawal.

55 R. Freeman Butts, "The Role of Civic Education in Rebuilding Education in Afghanistan," Teachers College Media Center from the Office of External Affairs (June 1, 2002).

http://www.tc.columbia.edu/news.htm?articleid=4841.

56 Teachers College, Columbia University, Series 66, April 1975, p. 223 (funding on these projects was from the Agency for International Development [AID] of the U.S. Department of

State).

Note: Freeman Butts and I served together on the Teachers College faculty in the 1970s. I remember the Afghan Project as primarily a "democratization through education" effort. Faculty chatter suggested an intelligence connection. We also knew it as a remote assignment for faculty with issues.

57   http://understandingwar.org/afghanistan.

58   https://en.m.wikipedia.org/wiki/shock_and_awe.

59   http://www.wsj.com/articles/ash-carter-offers-peek-at-2017-pentagon-budget-1454424118.

60   https://en.m.wikipedia.org/wiki/battle_of_mogadishu_(2006).

61   http://www.cbsnews.com/news/navy-seals-abort-mission-to-capture-al-shabaab-leader-in-Somalia.

62   www.telegraph.co.uk/news/worldnews/africaandindianocean/somalia/12186750/.

63   Robert Wright, "ISIS and the Forgotten, Deadly Threat of Homegrown Terrorism," *The Atlantic*, September 19, 2014.

64   "The African Terror Front," *Wall Street Journal*, March 16, 2016, A-14.

65   http://www.foreignpolicy.com/2014/08/28/found-the-islamic-states-terror-laptop-of-doom/.

66   ibid, foreign policy.com

67   David Garrahan, "Empathy in the Counseling Process," *Journal of N.Y. School Counselor* Vol.2, No.1 (1968), 5.

68   Ted Koppel, *Lights Out: A Cyberattack, a Nation Unprepared, Surviving the Aftermath* (New York: Penguin Random House, 2015).

69   Rush H. Limbaugh, *See, I Told You So* (New York: Pocket Books / Simon & Schuster, 1993), 257.

70   Bill Wanlund, "Intelligence Reform: Are U.S. Spy Agencies Prepared for 21st-Century Threats?" www.library.cqpress.com/cqresearcher/document.php?id=cqresrre2015052900&type=hitlist&n.

71 https://www.gao.gov/products/gao-16-294.

72 Will Hurd, "The Data Breach You Haven't Heard About," *Wall Street Journal*, January 27, 2016, A-11.

73 http://computerworld.com/article/2983749/cybercrime-hacking/ attackers-hacked-deptofenergy-159-times-in-4years.html
Richard A. Clarke and Robert K. Knake, *Cyber War: The Next Threat to National Security and What to Do about It* (New York: Harper Collins, 2010).

74 John D. Woodward Jr., "Sharing Fingerprints and DNA in the Antiterror Fight," *Wall Street Journal*, January 13, 2016.

75 Mike Pompeo and David B. Rivkin, Jr., "Time for Rigorous National Debate about Surveillance," *Wall Street Journal*, January 4, 2016, A-15.

76 www.theguardian.com/technology/2016/feb/05/twitter-deletes-isis-accounts-terrorism.

77 http://www.theguardian.com/world/2013/oct/23/us-monitored-angela-merkel-german-chancellor.
Related: Adam Entous and Danny Yadron, "U.S. Spying Nabs Allies: Israel, Germany, France, Even American Lawmakers Are Swept Up in N.S.A. Net," *Wall Street Journal*, December 30, 2015.

78 https://www.ice.gov.

79 https://www.ice/removal-statistics.

80 Ibid.

81 Paul Bedard, "ICE: 124 Illegal Immigrants Released from Jail Later Charged in 138 Murder Cases," *Politics*, March 14, 2016. http://www.foxnews.com/politics/2016/03/14/ice-124-illegal-im migrants-released-from-jail-later-later-charged-in-138-murder-cases.

82 http://www.usace.army.mil/about.aspx.

83 http://www.usace.army.mil/about/history/brief-historyofthe corps/respondingtoneeds.aspx.

84 Note: It is my expectation that after initial incidents, this authorization would be exercised infrequently.

85 http://www.cbs.ca/beta/news/canada/the-canada-u-s-border-by-the-numbers-1.999207.

86 http://www.cnsnews.com/new/article/canadian-border-bigger-terror-threat-Mexican-border-says-border-patrol-chief, May 18, 2011.

87 Ibid.

88 Ibid.

89 http://fronterasdesk.org/greater-US-security-threat-mexican-or-canadianborder.

90 http://heritage.org/research.

91 http://www.theguardian.com/US -news/2015/nov/17/richard-burr-visitors-without-visas-worse-than-refugees.

92 http://help.cbp.gov/app/answers/detail/a_id/194/~/visa-waiver-program-update.

93 http://workpermit.com/us/green_card_lottery.

94 "The Cost of Mass Deportation," *Wall Street Journal*, March 19–20, 2016, A12

95 http://www.pewhispanic.org/Files/2014/11/2014 -11-18_unauthorized_immigration.pdf.

96 "The Cost of Mass Deportation," *Wall Street Journal*, March 19–20, 2016, A12.

Chapter Four
Resetting Foreign Policy and Refocusing the Military

97 https://www.nationalpriorities.org/works-on/military-security/.

98 National Intelligence Council Report, *Global Trends 2025: A Transformed World* (Washington, DC: US Government Printing Office, 2008).

99 http://www.dni.gov/index.php.
    Note: ODNI agencies include the CIA, DIA, DHS, DEA, TBI, NSA, Departments of State, Treasury, Energy (readers can read the complete list and reports at the DNI website).

100 https://www.washingtonpost.com/news/worldviews/

wp/2012/12/11/the-coming-rise-and-decline-of-world-powers-foretold-in-charts/.

101 https://www.eisenhower.archives.gov/research/online _documents/farewell_address.html.

Note: the complete final text can be read at: Avalon.law.yale. edu/20th_century/eisenhower001.asp.

102 https://en.m.wikipedia.org/wiki/United_States _withdrawal_from_the_United_Nations.

103 Brett D. Schaefer, "America, We Pay Way Too Much for the United Nations," June 16, 2015, http://foxnews.com/opinion/2015/06/16/ America-pay-way-too-much-for-united-nations.html.

104 Note: UN members with diplomat car plates continue to park illegally throughout NYC and owe the city sixteen million dollars in unpaid parking fines.

105 Foxnews.com.

https://wikipedia.org/wiki/United_States_and _the_United-Nations.

106 https://www.debate.org/opinions/US-withdrawal-from-the-United-Nations-should-the-United-States-withdraw-from-the-U-N.

107 Senator Robert Torricelli and Andrew Carroll, *In Our Words* (New York: Kodansha America, 1999), 296–297.

108 Benjamin H. Friedman and Christopher Preble, "Refocusing U.S. Defense Strategy," http://www.downsizinggovernment.org/ defense/refocusing-us-defense-strategy.

109 https://www.bbc.com/news/world-middle-east-34912581.

110 http://www.theguardian.com/world/2015/oct/08/north-korea-could-hit-us-homeland-with-nuclear-weapon-say-top-admiral.

111 http://www.defense.news.com/story/defense/international/ americas/2016/01/04/pentagon-reason-russia-view-us-threat/78280396/.

112 http://www.breitbart.com/national-security/2015/08/06/ report-russian-hacked-on-pentagon-the-most-sophisticated-in-

military-history.

113 Note: Fifty years ago, I was recruited by the military because of my Russian lineage and familiarity with the language. About twenty husband-wife teams were selected for Russian-language training. I assume that the State Department has diplomats with this training in 2016.

114 David Vine, "The United States Probably Has More Foreign Military Bases than Any Other People, Nation, or Empire in History: and It's Doing Us More Harm than Good," *The Nation*, September 14, 2015.

115 Devlin Barrett and Gordon Lubold, "Officials Doubt Charges for U.S. Missile in Cuba," *Wall Street Journal*, January 9–10, 2016.

116 Mackenzie Eaglen, "Tech-Challenged Pentagon Searches for a Silicon Ally," *Wall Street Journal*, February 1, 2016, www.AEI.org/publication/tech-challenged-pentagon-searches-for-a-silicon-ally/.

117 http://www.bbc.com/news/world-asia-35526260.

118 http://www.heritage.org/research/reports/2015/06/south-korea-needs-thaad-missile-defense.

119 http://www.defense.gov/news/news-transcripts/transcript-view/article/654038/department-of-defense-briefing-by-vice-admiral-syring.

120 http://www.defenseindustrydaily.com/3979m-next-step-or-last-step-for-gmd-05229.

121 Mead Gruver, "New Air Force ICBM Commander: Cultural Change Will Continue," *Associated Press*, November 16, 2015.

122 Dan Caldwell, "GOP Candidates Need to Focus More on Waste and Inefficiency in Defense Budget," *The Hill*, February 5, 2016, www.thehill.com/blogs/congress-blog/presidentialcampaign/268294.

Chapter Five
Economic Revitalization and Available Health Care

123 http://www.gobankingrates.com/savings-account-average-ac

count-interest-rate.

124 Edwin Meese III, *With Reagan: The Inside Story* (Washington, DC: Regnery Gateway, 1992), 86–87.

Jon Huntsman and Tim Roemer, http://www.politco.com/magazine/story/2015/10/how-money-poisons-our-politics-213298.

125 Edwin Meese III, *With Reagan: The Inside Story* (Washington, DC: Regnery Gateway, 1992).

126 http://www.gallup.com/poll/185759/widespread-government-corruption.aspx.

127 www.hhs.gov/about/budget/fy2015/budget-in-brief/ihs/index.html.

Indian Health Service (.gov) documents. (This gov site is 212 pages, and the dollar amounts are slightly different.)

128 E. W.Gordon, David P. Garrahan, et al, *Report of the Study of Collegiate Compensatory Programs for Disadvantaged Youth* (New York: Ford Foundation, 1972), 525.

Garrahan authored the sections on Native Americans and Chicanos (pp. 27–41) and was solely responsible for the final reduction, analyses, and summarization of all survey data.

129 www.indiancountrytodaymedianetwork.com/2016/02/10/across-the-board-increases-obamas-indian-country-budget-163371.

130 http://ncela.ed.gov/rcd/bibliography/BE023773.
Darek Hunt, "BIA's Impact on Indian Education Is Bad Education," (http://indiancountrytodaymedianetwork.com/2012/01/30/bia's-impact-indian-education-is-bad-education-75083.

131 Grigg W. Moran and M. Kuang, "National Indian Education Study 2009," National Assessment of Educational Progress, United States Deparment of Education (June 2010).

132 Darek Hunt, "BIA's Impact on Indian Education Is Bad Education," (http://indiancountrytodaymedianetwork.com/2012/01/30/bia's-impact-indian-education-is-bad-education-75083.

133 Garrahan on Indian education: "In 1969, I was a founding member

of the National Association for Minorities Education (NAME). As a non-profit, we sought legal counsel, but were not able to find a Native American attorney in Oklahoma. Understandable in 1969.

134 Richard J. Herrstein and Charles Murray, *The Bell Curve: Intelligence and Class Structure in American Life* (New York: Free Press, 1994), 845.

135 Kimberly Teehee, speech before the UN Permanent Forum on Indigenous Issues in NYC, May 16, 2011, http://usun.state.gov/remarks/5058.

136 "In 1996, I applied for a position in education with the Yavapai Tribe in Arizona. Their reservation straddled Prescott where my home was located. I offered to work the first year without pay. I was not granted an interview. My resume noted that I had been twice recognized in Washington for my educational leadership. The second visit was in recognition of my substance use prevention research."

137 *A Quiet Crisis: Federal Funding and Unmet Needs in Indian Country* (Washington, DC: US Commission on Civil Rights, 2003.

138 Bentson H. McFarland, Roy M. Gabriel, Douglas A. Bigelow, and Dale Walker, "Organization and Financing of Alcohol and Substance Abuse Programs for American Indians and Alaska Natives," *American Journal of Public Health* 96, No. 8 (August 2006): 1469.

139 Garrahan, David, "The Application of a Systems Approach to Substance Use Prevention: Linking Interventions to the Infrastructure," *Journal of Alcohol and Drug Education* Vol.40, No.3 (Spring 1995).

140 Edwards, Chris, "Downsizing the Federal Government: Indian Lands, Indian Subsidies, and the BIA," www.downsizinggovernment.org/interior/indian-lands-indian-subsidies-and-the-BIA. *Journal of Indian Education* Vol.45, Issue 3 (2006).

141 https://en.m.wikipedia.org/wiki/list-of-federal-

agencies_in_the_U_S.
https://CEI.org/blog/nobody-knows-how-many-federal-agen
cies-exist.

142 https://en.m.wikipedia.org/wiki/united_states
_institute_of_peace.

143 http://NewYorkTimes.com/1990/12/31/US/still-no-end-to-the-
turmoil-at-legal-services.html.
(also) https://en.m.wikipedia.org/wiki/legal_services_corporation
_#grant_recipients.

144 https://en.m.wikipedia.org/wiki/national_endowment
_for_Democracy_#criticisms.

145 http://cato.org/publications/foreign-policy-briefing/loose-can
non-national-endowment-democracy.

146 https://en.m.wikipedia.org/wiki/2015/gold_kiing
_mine_waste_water_spill#epa_foreknowledge.

147 https://en.m.wikipedia.org/wiki/Flint_water_crisis
#early_water_contamination.

148 Wall Street Journal, Editorial, March 18, 2016, p. A-10.

149 Kelly, John and Mark Nichols, "How USA Today ID'ed Water
with High Lead Levels," *USA Today*.

150 www.USAtoday.com/story/news/nation/2016/03/16/how-water-
systems-identified/81281.

151 Newkirk, Barrett, *The Desert Sun*, Palm Springs, March 16, 2016.

152 Mark Levin, *Plunder and Deceit: Big Government's Exploitation
of Young People and the Future* (New York: Threshold Editions,
Simon and Schuster, 2015), 51.

153 https://www.cbpp.org/research/social-security/policy-basics-top-
ten-facts-about-social-security.

154 https://www.cbo.gov/publication/49795.

155 https://ssa.gov/disability/.

156 http://www.heritage.org/research/reports/2014/11/
triple-dipping-thousands-of-veterans-receive-more-than-
$100,000-in-benefits-every-year.

157 https://en.m.wikipedia.org/wiki/black-lung-benefits-act-of-1973.

158 Note (personal knowledge): One man living in NYC and working full-time as a longshoreman on the docks loading cargo on ships received his black lung check at his NYC home and later at his Florida home until age ninety-six. Another man, a veteran, would rub his arms vigorously with a bar of homemade brown soap before driving to his VA medical recertification exam. This was years after his dermatological condition had been cured.

159 http://www.quoteaddicts.com/465576.

160 Catey Hill, "45% of Americans Pay No Federal Income tax," MarketWatch, February 29, 2016, http://www.marketwatch.com/story/45-of-americans-pay-no-federal-income-tax-2016-02-24.

161 http://www.taxfoundation.org/article/details-and-analysis-senator-ted-cruz-s-tax-plan.

162 http://www.nytimes.com/2014/09/14/your-money-jeers-and-cheers-over-tax-inversions.
Jeff Sommer, "Jeers and Cheers over Tax Inversions," *New York Times*, September 13, 2014.

163 http://www.Americansfortaxfairness.org/tax-dodging-corporations.

164 http://www.wsj.com/articles/American-tax-exceptionalism-1443387986.

165 http://www.forbes.com/sites/jasonnazar/2013/09/09/16-surprising-statistics-about-small-businesses/.

166 Greg Ip, "Powerful Pair: Presidency and Protectionism," *Wall Street Journal*, March 10, 2016, A-2.

167 Robert Restor and Rachel Sheffield, "Setting Priorities for Welfare Reform," The Heritage Foundation, issue brief no. 4520, http://www.heritage.org/research/reports/2016/02/setting-priorities-for-wefare-reform.

168 Ibid.

169 Personal note: Learned to be independent at age seven (mother in mental hospital, father gone). Learned which grocery stores

and lunch shops had the best garbage, which churches were good to sleep in (and had the best poor boxes), which were the best corners to hawk newspapers. Built a shoeshine box from a fruit box. Learned when office workers got out of work, followed the leather shoes, even into bars, and quickly had a pub-shine-only business. I learned about independence and not having to beg or steal, but I failed first grade.

170 Robert Restor and Rachel Sheffield, "Setting Priorities for Welfare Reform," The Heritage Foundation, issue brief no. 4520, http://www.heritage.org/research/reports/2016/02/setting-priorities-for-wefare-reform.

171 Martin D. Brown and Rachel Sheffield, "The Moynihan Report 50 Years Later: Why Marriage More than Ever Promotes Opportunity for All," http://heritage.org/research/reports/2015/03/the-Moynihan-report.

172 https://en.m.wikipedia.org/wiki/community_health_centers_in_the_United_States.
http://www.NACHC.com/hc-capital-development.CFM.

173 http://www.hhs.gov/opa/title-x-family-planning/.

174 http://kff.org/other/state-indicator/total-rural-health-clinics/.
http://www.HRSA.gov.

175 http://www.AHA.ORG/About/index.shtml.

176 Michael D. Tanner, "The American Welfare State: How We Spend Nearly $1 Trillion a Year Fighting Poverty—and Fail," CA to Institute, http://www.cato.org/publications/policy-analysis/american-welfare-state.

177 https://www.doleta.gov/budget.

178 http://frac.org/leg-act-center/budget-and-appropriations/budget-analysis.

179 https://www.whitehouse.gov/the-press-office/2016/02/09/fact-sheet-administrations-drug-control-budget.

180 https://www.goodreads.com/author/quotes/3543.Ronald_Reagan.

Chapter Six
Educating Americans

181 Garrahan was acknowledged as a contributor to the report of the Quality Education Commission, "All Our Children: A Vision for N.J. Schools in the 21ᵗʰ Century," 1991, 51 (Eric Document reference: ED356543-1, EA024798).
David Garrahan, A Bold New Reform for 2000,The Record, Vol.101, No.14,p.10,June 20,1995.

182 Readers who want to examine the data in depth can access the reports directly: http://nces.Ed.gov/nationsreportcard/subjectareas.aspx.

183 https://www.oecd.org/pisa/keyfindings/pisa-2012-results.htm.
US Department of Education, National Center for Education Statistics (2015), The Condition of Education 2015 (NCES 2015-144), International Assessments.

184 https://en.m.wikipedia.org/wiki/a_nation_at_Risk.

185 http://www2.ed.gov/about/overview/fed/10facts/index.html.

186 D.Garrahan, the Relationship Between Social Activism and Feelings of Powerlessness Among Low Socioeconomic College Students. Journal of College Student Personnel, Vol.15,No.2,pp.120-124,March, 1974.
D.GarrahanAn Analysis of the Relationship Between Feelings of Powerlessness and the Success of Socially Disadvantaged Students in Higher Education.Teachers College, Columbia University, 1972.
D.Garrahan.Report on the Status of Minority Programs in Higher Education, College Entrance Examination Board, New York, N.Y.1972.
D.Garrahan.Higher Education for Poor and Minority Youth:The State of Affairs, CEEB,National Emergency Conference, Yellow Springs, Ohio, Sept.1970.

187 http://www.ed.gov/news/press-releases/obama-2016-budget-seeks-expand-educational-opportunity-all-students.

188 http://atlas.newamerica.org/education-federal-budget.

189 David Garrahan and Merrcina Simeonidis, "Partners in Education: A 10-Year Success Story of Intergenerational Cooperation and Learning—Involving Preschoolers, H.S. teenagers, Community Volunteers, Parents, and Teachers," *School Leader* Vol.17, No.7 (September/October 1988): 36–48.

190 Note: The above referenced program was the course of study for Child Development I and II for twelfth-grade students. Topics included being a parent, single parenting, and child development. Students used the Peabody Language Development Kit and involved their preschoolers in hands-on experiences with pets and plants. Seniors maintained weekly records on each child's mastery of skills. We knew the program was successful when former students living in the community enrolled their own children in the program years later.

191 http://m.her.oxfordjournals.org/content/18/2/237.short. http://onlinelibrary.wiley.com/doi/10.1111/j.1746-1561.1986.tb05775.x/Abstract.

192 Garrahan, "Implementing a School Security Program," *Perspective* Vol.6, No.1 (Spring 1989): 13–14.

193 Note: During the initial three months, security recorded thirty-three violations, including the arrest of individuals from outside the district, each of whom had a record for selling drugs. We then initiated a substance-use prevention program, and after three years, we had evidence of a reduction in drug use and an increase in student achievement and enrollment in advanced-placement courses. In 1994, we were recognized in Washington as a drug-free school.

194 Rush Limbaugh, *See, I Told You So* (New York: Pocket Books of Simon & Schuster, 1993), 188.

195 David Garrahan, "Healing a 'Sick' System: Disjointed Education Reform Efforts Need the Salve of Unity to Succeed," *School Leader* Vol.24, No.5 (March/April 1994): 32–50.

196 Ibid., 32.

197 Ibid., 50.

198 Note: the closest I came to honoring the principle of no tenure was to serve as a district school superintendent for ten years without any contract.

199 David Garrahan, "Education's Most Sacred Cow," *School Leader* Vol.24, No.1 (July/August 1994): 27–29 and 42–43.
Garrahan and James L. Plosia, "Times Up for Teacher Tenure," *New Jersey Reporter* Vol.25, No.1 (May/June 1995).
Garrahan, "Superintendent Opposed to Tenure," *Town Journal* Vol.18, No.3 (May 16, 1991).

200 David Garrahan, "Monitoring and School Deregulation," *School Leader* Vol.19, No.6 (May/June 1990): 26–29, 43.

201 http://www.usnews.com/news/articles/2014/11/03/number-of-us-charter-schools-up-7-percent-report-shows.

202 https://NCES.ed.gov/fastfacts/display.asp.

203 David Garrahan, "Friends of the East Harlem Block Schools," *Concern* Vol.10, No.5 (February 1971): 4–5.

204 http://educationnext.org/teachers-unions-common-core/.
Alexander Russo, "Teachers Unions and the Common Core," *Education Next* Vol.15, No.1 (Winter 2015).

205 https://thecommoncore.wordpress.com/commoncore-arguments-for-and-against/.

206 D.Garrahan, Regionalization and the Organizational Transformation of Education, Perspective, Vol.8, No.4. pp.27-31, Winter, 1992.

207 Scott Jaschik, "New Sheriff in Town" (January 21, 2013),.www.insidehighereducation.com/news/2013/01/21/new-Purdue-president-outlines-critiques-higher-education.
Richard Arum and Josipa Roksa, *Academically Adrift: Limited Learning on College Campuses.*

208 Jordan Weissmann, "Here's Exactly How Many College Graduates Live Back at Home," *The Atlantic* (February 26, 2013),

http://www.theatlantic.com/business/archieve/2013/02/
here'sexactlyhowmanycollegegraduateslivebackathome.

209 Jeffery Sparshott, "Congratulations, Class of 2015: You Are the Most Indebted Ever," *Wall Street Journal* (May 8, 2015).

210 http://collegedebt.com/.

211 Jorge Klor de Alva and Mark Schneider, "The Feds and Students vs. Taxpayers," *Wall Street Journal* (March 4, 2016): A-13.

212 Note: I washed dishes and worked in the college library. Walking out of my dormitory, the dean asked me what I was doing on campus. I replied that I didn't know that colleges close on Thanksgiving. "Go home, Garrahan." "But I don't have a home." He phoned his wife and told me that I could stay with them but had better find somewhere to go for Christmas. Later, my English professor drove me to his dentist and paid to have a set of teeth made for me. I graduated in three and a half years and began teaching physics, chemistry, and algebra. Earned a master's degree at Lehigh University and additional graduate credits at the University of Scranton, Rutgers University, Cornell University, NYU and a doctorate from Columbia University in NYC post doctorate certification Institute for Advanced Study of Rational Psychotherapy (direct supervision by Albert Ellis). My children were five, six, and seven years of age. Returned to my grade school to find out why I failed first grade.

213 David Garrahan, *Affirmative Action Compliance* (Rochester: Title IX Conference, March 9, 1977).

214 David Garrahan, "In Support of Recruiting Negroes," *The Pocono Record*, April 1970, Editorial page.

215 David Garrahan, "Sex Equality in Educational and Vocational Guidance," APGA, Washington, March 1978, Abstracts No. 494, 70 and 198.

216 Note: Taking a position to chair a university department in 1977, I found my faculty scattered in buildings across the campus. I reassigned them offices in one location, more accessible to students.

They could interact with colleagues and create a departmental identity and a battle royal.

Chapter Seven
Action Guide to Transition America

217 www.westillholdthesetruths.org/quotes/2188/either-you-will-control-your-government.
218 www.archives.gov/federal register/constitution/article-V.html.

Epilogue

219 David Garrahan, "Helping the Forgotten Students in Our Schools," New Jersey Association of HS Councils, Yearbook, June 1962, 94–96.
220 David Garrahan, "Gerontological Counseling: A Developmental Life Stage Approach," *New Jersey Journal of Professional Counseling* Vol.49, No.1 (Spring 1986): 4–6.

And on a lighter note, U.S. Senator Jon Corzine
and the author celebrate birthdays!